Contents

Introduction

Today's kitchen is one of the busiest multipurpose rooms in a home. Not only does it see a lot of foot traffic, it also serves many different roles at different times. It may be a place to prepare food in the morning and evening, but can also be a place to eat a leisurely (or not so leisurely) meal, a workroom to tackle homework and bills, and a conference center for family meetings. And, more than ever, today's kitchen is the home's social center, where friends and family gather to relax and share down time. The best kitchen design not only accounts for all these different roles, it actually enhances them and makes them more pleasurable.

That's a lot to ask from any room design, especially one in which comfort is king. Fortunately, you've never had a broader range and diversity of kitchen design elements from which to choose. Surface options alone—materials to clad the floors, countertops, backsplashes, and walls—are offered in a head-spinning number of variations. Choose the innate beauty and durability of natural quarry stone, the latest exciting versions of inexpensive laminates, or from among a bevy of recycled materials that will ensure your kitchen is as "green" as possible. And green isn't just a movement; it's one of a rainbow of hues included as surface options.

The ongoing trend toward more color in this traditionally neutral-colored space has led to all kinds of new and exciting looks. Large appliances, tiles, fixtures, and cabinetry are all offered in eye-catching colors. The bolder hues popular a few years ago have given way to a somewhat subtler palette, but the desire of homeowners to introduce more color into their kitchens continues unabated.

SPEND A LITTLE MORE FOR SMALL DETAILS. A modest bump in price can mean that surfaces look more upscale and bring the investment back to you in spades. The laminate countertop shown here already has a beautiful faux-marble surface, but an "ogee" edge profile puts the icing on the cake of the illusion. It looks remarkably like the profile on a real stone countertop, for a fraction of the cost. An ogee profile is a great way to create a perception of opulence in your kitchen countertops, regardless of what the actual material may be.

That color needs to be illuminated, and newer LED fixtures are changing the way we look at our kitchens—at least when the sun is down. An ever-expanding array of lighting fixture designs gives us more ways than ever to properly illuminate the well-designed kitchen (and that's not even counting tubular skylights that are bringing brilliant sunlight to formerly dim rooms).

All this means that you won't hurt for a multitude of options—whether you're looking to completely remodel your kitchen or just update it a bit with one or two modest touches. There is nothing like an embarrassment of riches to spur the imagination, and the imagination is the tool of choice when you want to create a usable, beautiful kitchen in your own signature style.

IMPRESS WITH SUBTLE ELEGANCE. You don't necessarily need bold colors or sleek surfaces to create a killer kitchen design. Here, accents like a gooseneck faucet and island-mounted pot filler accent the sophisticated cream-colored cabinets and the matching face panels on the refrigerator. The butcher block, marble counters, and inset cooktop drive home the point that this is a serious cook's kitchen, but one with a refined aesthetic sense.

USE YOUR APPLIANCES TO MAKE A STATEMENT. There's no excuse for dull appliances in a newly designed or renovated kitchen. Today, manufacturers offer units that combine exceptional function with unusual looks. This glass front refrigerator is just one example, but a sleek one that makes sense for a stunning cooking-oriented kitchen. You get a peek in at what's on offer without ever opening the door—translating to energy savings and a cool visual.

CREATE A PERSONALIZED ACCENT WITH A BACKSPLASH. Here, fun and colorful mosaic glass tile creates an upbeat look that brings a little zest to the otherwise stately look of a stainless steel hood, professional-quality range, and traditional cabinets. Backsplashes are the dream canvases of a kitchen, where you can get a bit wild without risking too much.

EXPERIMENT WITH KITCHEN COLOR BY PAINTING THE WALLS. Muted kitchen colors are all the rage, but fashion and tastes change, and paint can change with them. Notice how well this particular color works with the elegant granite counters and the traditional, raised-panel, framed cabinets. The cabinets feature a rich maple finish that would complement a wide range of colors, and the same is true of the stainless steel appliances.

DECORATE WITH FUNCTION. The right kitchen fixture in the right place adds wonderfully to the look of the room, but also makes the space more efficient and easier to use. Here, a wall-mounted pot filler faucet folds up out of the way when not in use, and offers a quick and convenient water source for cooking when needed. The gleaming modern form of the fixture adds a spot of style in an unexpected place.

USE LIGHT FIXTURES AS SIGNATURE DESIGN ELEMENTS. The wealth of lighting options offered by today's lighting manufacturers means you can find eye-catching fixtures to suit just about any kitchen design style—even as a standalone design feature that announces your aesthetic intentions. This curving halogen track contrasts the straight lines that otherwise dominate the room, and a row of understated pendants hangs from the same track. It's a mix of illuminating styles in one fixture.

INCORPORATE SMALL, ELEGANT DETAILS AS KITCHEN JEWELRY. Pulls, knobs, and handles are all opportunities to get big design bang for your remodeling dollar. Stylish handles such as the silver-toned sleek models accenting this black cabinet door can make or break the overall look of cabinetry. If design dynamite comes in small packages, kitchen cabinetry hardware is pure TNT.

OPT FOR ECO-FRIENDLY UPCALE. A bamboo island and reclaimed flagstone wall cladding are environmentally friendly design options that bring a stunning complement to luxury appliances in this kitchen. The sleek stainless steel exterior of the appliances and the sophisticated smoked-glass window fronting the wine refrigerator are perfect contrasts to the rough-hewn surface of the walls. This type of textural contrast is a great way to build visual interest in your kitchen.

THINK "UNUSUAL MATERIALS" TO CREATE CENTERPIECE SURFACES. This work surface was custom-formed of float glass and then set into a concrete frame. This is a truly modern look, but one with an enchantingly industrial edge. Regardless of the style tag you stick on it, this idea could be adapted to many different kitchen decorating styles. The homeowner could have chosen from among a spectrum of glass colors, and the concrete can be tinted, polished to a high sheen, or even stamped with a unique surface relief.

ADD A FARMHOUSE SINK FOR COUNTRY FLAIR.
Country or farmhouse kitchen designs are often
defined by a few key design elements, one of which
is the enameled cast iron apron-front farmhouse sink.
Its distinctive profile is unmistakable, and the form
of the sink provides plenty of room inside to clean
and maneuver oversized pots and pans. Match the
sink with a super stylish shiny chrome faucet like the
traditional gooseneck unit shown here, and you have an
unbeatable combination that brings a lot of pizazz to the
country kitchen.

GO MODERN ELECTRIC FOR SPECTACULAR
STREAMLINED APPEARANCES. Today's induction
electric cooktops give any gas units a run for their
money in both looks and performance. A high-end
electric cooktop like this one simply can't be topped
for a sleek, minimalist look. Paired with a stunning
range hood like the glass-edged model in this kitchen, a
modern electric cooktop can be a big style focal point in
a modern or contemporary kitchen design.

Style by Size

Bringing your own kitchen design vision to life entails many considerations—the room's social uses, the practical aspects of how you prefer to prepare and cook food, the home's overall design style—but none have a greater impact than the physical size and layout of the space. In fact, the dimensions of the room may actually lead you toward one design style or another. For example, modern designs are best suited to an open floor plan and larger spaces; informal country styles work well in more modest kitchens.

In any case, unless you're adding onto your home or spending a small fortune changing the actual layout of the structure, you'll have to work within the confines of a predetermined space.

Start with the practical matters. Installing an island or moving cabinets is a big, expensive change that can alter the "work triangle" within your kitchen and make the kitchen more usable. But you can also make smaller alterations that perk up the look of the room and make it more comfortable for cooking, eating, and just sitting around socializing. The right lighting fixtures can make dark corners of a larger kitchen more user friendly and may even visually expand the space, while updated countertops can give any size kitchen a facelift.

You may not own a kitchen that is exactly the size and configuration you always envisioned, but that doesn't mean it can't be the perfect kitchen for you, your family, and friends. It's just a matter of making the most of the space you have and focusing on the high points and potential in the room.

GO SPLASHY IN SMALL SPACES. You can spend a little more where there is less area to cover—such as the solid surface, tiered quartz countertop and top-of-the-line stainless steel appliances used in this galley kitchen. The counter material is stronger than granite and every bit as handsome. Designer stools and spectacular hanging light fixtures round out a look that is the very height of small-space sophistication.

EXPLOIT THE WORK TRIANGLE. The triangle formed between the stove, sink/prep area, and refrigerator is the core of how efficient your kitchen will be. Experts call this the work triangle, and it should be as compact as possible to limit the number of steps you need to take from one area to the next. This compact kitchen includes an island sink that makes moving from food prep to cooktop as simple as turning around. Thoughtful layout like this is the key to any successful kitchen design, but is especially important in smaller rooms.

Cozy Kitchens

ADAPT TO NARROW KITCHENS. Small, narrow kitchens require creativity to make the most of the limited space. The cabinets and countertops in this tiny room are narrower than standard, to allow for as much open floor space as possible. The stove, refrigerator, and sink are perfectly positioned in relationship to one another to ensure economy of movement in the room. Glass cabinet fronts make it easy to find exactly what you're looking for.

USE CLUTTER FOR COMFORT IN A SMALL KITCHEN. As this kitchen layout shows, a small space doesn't necessarily need to be austere to be usable and welcoming. This cozy room uses a mix of open, vertical, and overhead storage to optimize every square inch. Although the kitchen appears to be jam packed, everything has a place, and it's easy to find whatever the cook might need. It's also a very homey look that seems both fun and comfortable.

LEVERAGE LIGHT TONES TO OPEN UP A SMALL KITCHEN. The lovely natural wood finish and simple lines of the wall and base cabinets, along with the timeless muted green of the island, help visually expand this modest kitchen. The same idea drove the choice of light pine for the flooring rather than darker oak or other wood, and bright white for the ceiling. It helps that the window has not been blocked by a window treatment and that the countertop surfaces are all light and bright as well.

BREAK THE WINDOW . . . RULES. In general, it's not a good idea to block a window with a structural element. But that rule can be bent if not broken, as this kitchen clearly shows. The designer has run open shelving across two double-hung windows. The operable part of the window is below where the shelf bisects the opening, allowing the window to function as it would otherwise. The design creates dynamic lines where you wouldn't expect them and allows the homeowner to store elegant vessels and cookware fully illuminated by the sun streaming through the windows. It's an unusual design tactic, but one that works well here.

FOCUS ON STANDOUT MATERIALS TO MAKE SMALL KITCHENS SPECIAL. The unforgettable zebrawood countertop in this kitchen provides stunning visual patterns and a rich, deep finish, serving as a centerpiece that contrasts the understated cabinetry and walls. Because the surface only needs to cover a small area, the expense was kept to a minimum while the eye appeal is at maximum. Exotic hardwoods offer a range of exceptional looks and long-term durability, making them ideal choices for special surfaces.

Family-Friendly Spaces

DESIGN SURFACES TO DO DOUBLE DUTY IN A BUSY FAMILY KITCHEN. The stepped-down tiered island in this room creates a surface that can host breakfast at one moment, and accommodate food preparation the next. The handsome countertops may look like two types of slate, but they are actually durable, convincing faux stone laminates that offer the beauty of stone at a more budget-friendly price. The choice of cherry finish on the cabinets is insightful for the busy kitchen: they are unlikely to ever look dingy or show wear.

SIZE THE ISLAND TO THE KITCHEN. An overlarge island in the wrong space becomes a barrier to efficiency and traffic movement, rather than an aid. This smart kitchen features an open island with easily accessible shelves, so there is no worry about door swing. The island is also smaller than usual, making it perfectly suited to a modestly sized family kitchen. The different countertop sets it apart from the other surfaces in the room and creates a lovely visual contrast.

EXPAND THE NOTION OF ISLANDS IN A FAMILY KITCHEN. A kitchen island can be many things. In this well-arranged kitchen, the extended island not only hosts the induction cooktop, it also stands in for a more traditional kitchen table. Handsome maple base cabinets match the cabinets used in the rest of the kitchen, effectively tying the look of this peninsula island to the kitchen as a whole. The light finish of the cabinets balances the effect of the nearly black floor and other gray elements, to create a look that's greater than the sum of its parts.

MAINTAIN VISUAL BALANCE TO CREATE A COMFORTABLE FAMILY KITCHEN. Here, white granite countertops contrast the ebony cabinets to create striking eye candy. The light, neutral-colored mosaic tiles split the difference between the two extremes. This kitchen also features cost-cutting luxury in countertops that are not solid granite, but a granite shell made from the leftover scraps of solid countertop production. There's really no way to tell the difference except when you pay the bill.

Family-Friendly Spaces

KEEP THINGS OPEN AND AIRY TO MAKE A MEDIUM-SIZE KITCHEN LOOK LARGER. The freestanding base cabinets in this kitchen, coupled with the light colors used throughout, glass fronted wall-mount cabinets, and an open floor plan, create a more spacious feel to the kitchen and give it a fresh aspect. Freestanding cabinets can open up any kitchen, although the look is less formal than other types of cabinetry.

EQUIP A BUSY FAMILY KITCHEN FOR ACTION. This medium-sized family social center comes outfitted for cooking big meals, with a restaurant-quality six-burner range and top and bottom wall-mounted ovens. Although this type of equipment may seem like a luxury, it can save a lot of time and frustration for the cook preparing meals in a busy kitchen. That's why large appliances are great places to splurge in any medium kitchen makeover.

CENTERPIECE ISLANDS MAKE FOR EFFICIENT KITCHENS. Using an island as the center of a busy family kitchen is a traditional layout technique that still works quite well. This island follows all the rules, being small enough to leave plenty of room for travel around the structure and big enough to serve multiple purposes—such as breakfast bar, prep surface, and open storage. It's also in keeping with the style of the kitchen.

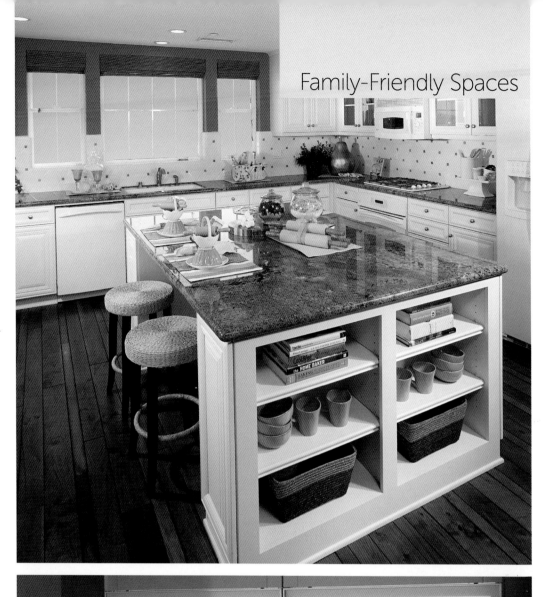

DESIGN AHEAD FOR EASY CLEANUP. Cleanable surfaces are key to keeping a busy mid-size kitchen looking its best at all times, with a minimum of effort. The square-edge solid surface countertops, glass tile backsplash, flat-front base cabinets, and glass fronted wall-mount cabinets are all easy to clean with a quick swipe. The sharp contemporary lines of all the kitchen's features ensure that there are no nooks and crannies in which dirt can hide.

MAKE A MODEST KITCHEN SEEM OPULENT WITH SPECIAL FIXTURES AND SURFACES. This modern kitchen isn't large but plays visually big thanks to a wealth of stunning, natural wood surfaces and sophisticated lighting that includes recessed ceiling lights, cabinet lighting, accent lights, and decorative lighting around the edge of the island countertop. The effect is one of super sophistication and polish and makes a big impact in a less-than-huge space.

ADD STYLE AND FUNCTION WITH CAREFULLY CHOSEN SPECIALTY FIXTURES. Fixtures such as the pot-filler faucet shown here are not essential to a kitchen, but make a busy family kitchen much more efficient. Incorporating a countertop-mount style ensures that the faucet is as good at drawing attention as it is at making pasta prep a quicker chore. Whenever you're thinking about a pot filler faucet, make sure that there is plenty of clearance all around so the function of the faucet is never blocked.

DISGUISE UTILITY FEATURES IN MEDIUM-SIZE KITCHENS. This trash compacter has been concealed behind a faux cabinet front that matches the base cabinets in the room. Although a stainless steel front would have been a more conventional treatment, there's nothing pretty about a trash compacter and hiding it makes a lot of design sense. Notice how the illusion is made convincing by the addition of a drawer handle and pull.

ADD STYLE AND STORAGE WITH DISTINCTIVE POT RACKS. The straight-bar unit shown here is rugged and well suited to a busy family kitchen and country or contemporary design. This fixture, like most pot racks, adds a handsome, eye-catching feature that reinforces the notion of the kitchen as workspace and provides a wealth of storage for large, unwieldy pots and pans. The best thing about pot racks like this is that you can position them right over workspaces, so your cookware is at your fingertips anytime you cook.

Large & Luxurious

FABRICATE SURFACES TO FOLLOW AN UNUSUAL FLOOR PLAN. Large kitchens often feature layouts in unorthodox shapes. Exploit the variations by incorporating islands and counters that echo the shape of the floor plan. This helps make the entire room more comfortable for the eye to follow, and it also aids in traffic flow through the space. The island in this large room was constructed following this principle, and it becomes a visual centerpiece with a striking mottled quartz surface that mimics the look of marble.

CENTRALIZE THE WORK SURFACE IN A LARGE KITCHEN. The long, large island in this warm and well-appointed kitchen not only hosts the induction cooktop, it also provides abundant prep area that can be accessed from all sides. It leaves plenty of room for multiple cooks to comfortably work in the same space. The island boasts a wealth of cabinetry that matches the surrounding wall and base units, and the look is both striking and informal.

DON'T BE AFRAID TO LET LARGER SPACES BREATHE. The number one mistake homeowners make when they have a large kitchen to work with is filling it with so much clutter and oversized furnishings that it actually looks small and cramped. This kitchen is an example of how to leave room while still equipping the kitchen with the necessities. A standalone work island under a hanging light provides plenty of workspace, while the upscale stainless steel appliances provide visual anchors around the room that leads the eye logically through the space. High-quality flooring finishes the look and emphasizes the largeness of the room in a good way.

OPTIMIZE AN ISLAND IN A LARGE KITCHEN. When you have a lot of space to work with, you can expand the definition of an island and create a visual and gathering center point in the kitchen. This island is not only sized to provide a large, easily accessible work and dining surface, the faux marble laminate is a different style than the surrounding countertops. The surface, along with two high-style chandeliers, sets the island apart from the rest of the kitchen and gives it a unique identity. This is a great way to add visual interest and usable surface space to a large kitchen.

ADD LUXURY WITH HIGH-END EQUIPMENT. A restaurant-quality addition like this side-by-side dual-oven range not only brings a whole lot of cooking power to your meal preparation, it adds bling to the room and basically shouts that some serious eats are going to be whipped up. A custom enclosure around the high-end refrigerator makes it look like a standalone Asian-style cabinet, adding yet another visual layer to the look of a purely stunning kitchen.

ACCENT A LARGE KITCHEN WITH ELEGANT DETAILS. Something as simple as a sophisticated countertop edge profile can have a big design impact. The tiered, ogee-style profile shown here is an eye-catching feature that helps define the space at large. The recycled glass countertop adds just as much fascination to the room. Details like this help make a large kitchen really special, becoming something much more than just a great big space in which to cook and eat.

ADD LUXURY TO A LARGE KITCHEN WITH HIGH-END EQUIPMENT. A restaurant-quality addition like this six-burner gas range not only brings a whole lot of cooking power to your meal preparation, it adds bling to the room and basically shouts that some serious eats are going to be whipped up. And although it's the poor craftsperson who blames their tools, deluxe appliances such as these can sometimes even spur more cooking and entertaining adventures and make a gourmet out of a weeknight cook.

GIVE FINE CABINETRY THE STAGE IT DESERVES. Fine cabinet detailing is a sign of luxury, especially elegant touches like the inner edge profiles of these classic cabinets. Exquisite details like the fluting, cornices, and dentil molding on the wall-mounted cabinets can be too busy and may overwhelm smaller kitchens. But used in a substantial space like this, they all combine to create a sophisticated classic look that does the oversized kitchen justice. The off-white color only adds to the appeal.

STORE IN PLAIN SIGHT TO ADD LIFE. The large visual space in a luxury kitchen can sometimes lead to a cold "empty" feel, but not if you use exposed storage. Add features such as the wall-mounted shelves, sleek hanging rods, and rolling island caddy in this kitchen, and you provide delight for the eye. The dishes, cookware, and utensils all become graphic elements in their own right. But more to the point, they add a very human scale to the large space.

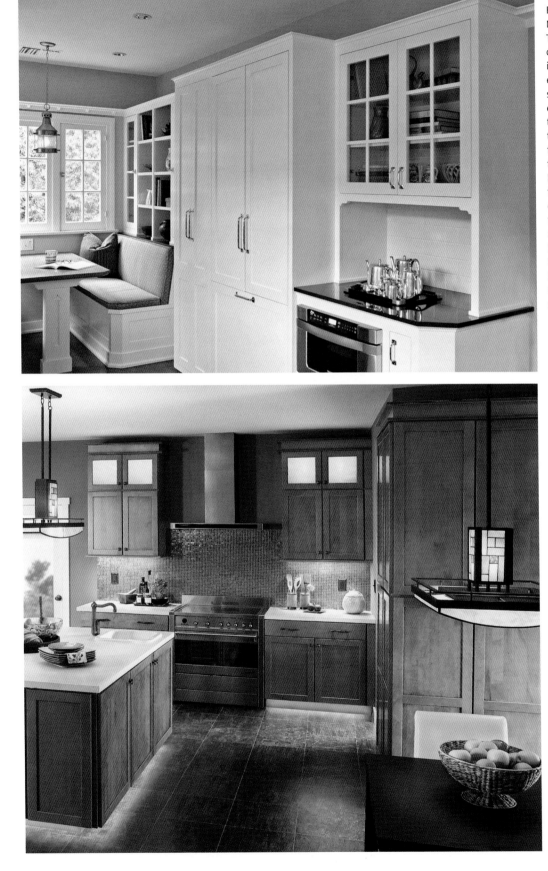

CUSTOMIZE LARGE ROOMS TO SUIT YOUR NEEDS AND TASTES. The extra space in an oversized luxury kitchen is an opportunity to put exactly the storage and structures you want, exactly where you want them. Here, for example, the homeowner has added floor-to-ceiling cabinets to store large items and has built in a kitchen table-and-banquette combination, complete with decorative wall shelving. The built-ins have been designed to match the cabinetry and molding throughout the room, seamlessly integrating the new structures.

SUPPLY A VARIETY OF LIGHTING TO PROPERLY SERVE LARGE KITCHENS. Sizeable luxury rooms host multiple roles, from a range of cooking and prepping chores, to large dinners, to family socializing, and beyond. All those activities require thoughtful lighting that also does the space justice. The lighting in this room includes craftsman style pendants, overhead fixtures, toe-kick lights for ease of navigation, and cabinet lights. Most are dimmable, and the mix of lighting ensures that any mood can be achieved and any task can be safely performed.

Scintillating Kitchen Styles

There's nothing to stop you from creating your own unique kitchen design style. But there's a good chance you'll be reinventing the wheel. You could far more easily put your own spin on one of the many established kitchen design styles, by using signature elements alongside the key indicators of whatever style appeals to you. Manufacturers create cabinets, flooring, countertops, appliances, and accessories specifically to suit well-known styles, so much of the work will already be done for you. However, making any style your own requires knowing a little bit about what does—and does not—define it. The descriptions that follow describe the most popular kitchen design styles. There are many variations on any theme, but these are good starting points in choosing a look that suits your tastes and your particular kitchen space.

- **Contemporary.** Bridging the divide between traditional and modern, contemporary kitchens feature "clean," minimal aesthetics with a lack of curving lines, flowing shapes, fussy elements, or ornate fixtures. However, contemporary rooms generally include a few key traditional design elements that help warm the space up a bit. The style is also constantly evolving, because it is literally about the "now." So it can include design elements that are trending in the moment, such as the muted colors popular these days.

- **Traditional.** A more formal style, traditional kitchens are characterized by symmetry and elaborate details. Dark cherry or mahogany cabinets may feature fluting, rosettes, corbels, built-up door panels, and dentil crown molding. Countertops will often have compound edge profiles, and the room can include complicated backsplash tile patterns such as diamonds. The style is all about intricate, sumptuous surfaces and elaborate fixtures.

- **Country, farmhouse, and cottage.** Turn to a country look for a more casual kitchen. This style is set apart by the use of simple, repetitive elements such as beadboard or faux beadboard cabinets and wall cladding.

RIFF ON ESTABLISHED STYLES WITH SIGNATURE FEATURES. The designer of this contemporary kitchen gave it an Asian flair with the addition of Ming red paint on the island cabinets, a relief design on a bank of wall-mounted cabinets, and a rice-paper overhead lighting fixture. The octagonal island shape and matching ceiling cutout ensure that this kitchen has an entirely unique feel beyond the particular design style.

SCREAM CONTEMPORARY WITH CLEAN LINES. Sleek and elegant lines like the clean edge of this solid surface counter, the simple shape of the sink, and futuristic L-shape of the ultra-cool faucet in this kitchen all reinforce the notion of "contemporary." Subtle and beautiful wall tiles and high-end frameless cabinets in dark bamboo add a bit of life and warmth to the room, softening the unyielding aspect of the crisp, uncomplicated lines.

USE GLASS TO DEFINE CONTEMPORARY. Glass surfaces are common to contemporary kitchens because they usually incorporate simple straight lines, unembellished edge profiles and a crisp, fresh look. The counters and wall tiles here bring a sparkle to the room that only glass can deliver. Frosted glass front cabinets add to the allure, and a new glass-front refrigerator carries through the theme in very cool fashion. Aside from the elegant and eye-catching look, glass surfaces make for quick and easy clean up.

Homey, rough-hewn materials come into play, such as tin backsplashes and ceilings and butcher block countertops. Farmhouse is a slightly more rustic variation, featuring certain key indicators like the apron-front "farmhouse" sink.

- **Modern.** Sleek, streamlined, and high-tech are all key points of this easily identified style. It's not for everyone or every kitchen—the look works best in larger spaces and open floor plans. The challenge is to institute a truly modern appeal without making the room seem overly cold or sterile. Judicious use of the occasional splash of color and incorporating natural textures such as hardwoods softens the sometimes stark visual nature.

Although these styles dominate kitchens throughout the country, they are by no means the only design styles from which you can choose. Others include historical styles such as Craftsman and Art Deco that hail from specific time frames, retro that can represent the curvy, colorful aspects of any of three decades (1950s, '60s, and '70s), and eclectic, which is the inspired use of seemingly disparate design elements that actually work together to create a unified look (easily the hardest style to make work). Choose your style based on what appeals to your design sense, meshes with your overall home design, and ultimately accommodates the way the room will be used.

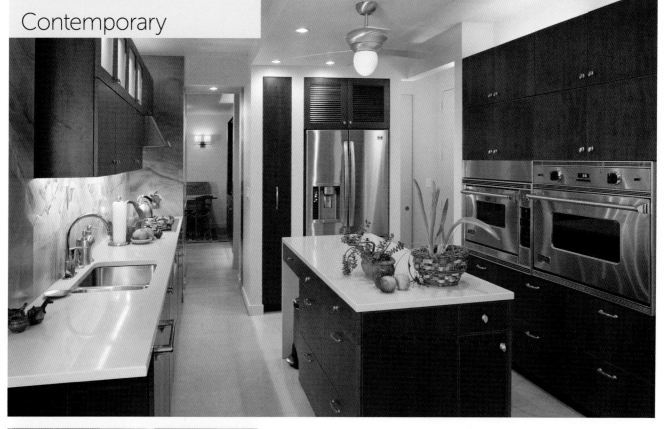

BALANCE LIGHT AND DARK FOR THE BEST CONTEMPORARY DESIGN. As this kitchen shows, a dynamic balance of darker design elements with light additions creates a visually satisfying tension in the room. The dark brown cabinets add a bit of gravitas to the room, while the solid-surface counters, lovely cork floor, and stainless steel appliances brighten the space and ensure that it doesn't feel too heavy or closed-in.

LIMIT COLOR IN CONTEMPORARY STYLE. A mix of hues creates too much visual noise for the calm and understated nature of a contemporary kitchen to really shine through. Color usage like the green in this contemporary kitchen is more appropriate; a dominant black-and-white scheme forms the base of the palette for the room, with points of visual pop provided by a basic mid-range green tone. The look is sophisticated and elegant, supplying color that pleases but doesn't overwhelm.

WARM UP CONTEMPORARY WITH A STUNNING SURFACE. The zebrawood used for this long island countertop brings a wealth of visual interest to a room that is otherwise comprised of straight lines, cream colors and plain design elements. Although the countertop may cost slightly more than more sedate options, choosing a special surface for a limited area like an island is a great way to get good bang for your buck without undermining the room's overall design style.

REINFORCE CONTEMPORARY STYLE WITH STAINLESS STEEL. The clean sharp appearance and lack of color or pattern make stainless steel a perfect surface material for just about any contemporary kitchen. The dual wall-mounted stoves, island counter, bullet pendant lights, and sink backsplash in this kitchen not only provide a sleek compliment to the bamboo cabinets, they also lead the eye through the kitchen's design.

CREATE MYSTERY WITH FROSTED GLASS. Frosted glass cabinet inserts achieve two kitchen design goals: they brighten the look with a sophisticated cabinet element, and they conceal what's inside, so that you don't have to worry about the artfulness of what you put in your cabinets. Frosted glass is also an ideal look for the minimal, sleek nature of a contemporary kitchen, and the material is on par with the cost of plain glass inserts.

LET CABINETS DEFINE THE ROOM. A great way to establish a style for your kitchen is by starting with the cabinets—the choice of which will drive other choices. Here, high-quality cherry cabinets set the stage for solid surface countertops and unique metal tiles with a relief surface design. The light tone of the cabinets provides relief for the eye and ties all the other elements together. Given the range of cabinet styles—from ready-to-assemble unadorned units, to totally over-the-top custom cabinets—it's easy to find exactly the look you want and build the rest of the design from there.

GO LINEAR TO EXPLOIT CONTEMPORARY STYLE. The open, floating shelves in this kitchen are the height of simplicity and they provide ample space for displaying attractive plates, glasses, and cookware. They also carry through a theme thick with lines, one that is echoed in the shape of the high-end range and the stunning patterns of the glass tile on the wall. Lines are an easy design point to build on in a contemporary kitchen.

CONFINE COLOR IN A CONTEMPORARY ROOM. Contemporary doesn't have to mean bland. You can use small bursts of color to add visual interest or put your own stamp on an otherwise subdued contemporary design. The designer of this room covered a small backsplash area with glass mosaic tiles in hot oranges and reds. The effect is minimalized because the feature can't be seen from everywhere in the kitchen and the square footage of the backsplash is limited. But it does bring a pulse-quickening bit of excitement to an otherwise low-key room.

Contemporary

MAKE A CONTEMPORARY DESIGN YOUR OWN. The homeowner who designed this kitchen began with modern materials, such as glass wall tile and stunning, 4-inch-thick black quartz countertops. Wood floors and cherry cabinetry warm the space up and lend a traditional element, while the lighting fixtures throughout add a bit of eclectic fun for the eye. It is a totally unique home design based on a contemporary foundation.

BORROW FREELY TO CREATE THE BEST CONTEMPORARY KITCHEN. The combination of traditional and modern is on full display in this cozy and visually interesting room. Traditional recessed door cabinets, fixtures, and wood flooring contrast with the bright orange modern stools and glitzy high-tech halogen track lights that follow the lines of the coffered ceiling. Using chalkboard paint as a stove backsplash surfacing is an inspired choice creating a changeable graphic in the room.

LET FIXTURES AND APPLIANCES DEFINE CONTEMPORARY. This large, open floor plan kitchen and dining area includes a state-of-the-art refrigerator with a door window, a pro-quality range with industrial hood, and stunning, one-of-a-kind of lighting fixtures that tie the dining and kitchen areas together. All feature modern technology in contrast to the more traditional cabinetry and upholstered chairs. A huge, freestanding, custom-made island screams "special" and adds to the overall look.

LEVERAGE CONTRAST. Part of what separates contemporary from modern and traditional kitchens is the use of clearly contrasting design elements to create a bit of visual tension. Here, the ornate backsplash tile pattern plays against the strong simple straight lines in the cabinetry. The engineered stone surface of the island countertop contrasts the warm wood floor and the soft upholstered chairs. It's a look that maintains visual interest without overwhelming the design with busy details.

MIX TO BLEND IN TRADITIONAL KITCHEN COLOR SCHEMES. Traditional style dictates neutral colors, but nothing says you need to make the entire scheme one neutral color. In addition to highly detailed glass-front cabinets featuring curving bentwood muntins, this kitchen alternates between grey cabinets and cabinets and architectural flourishes in bright white. The mix is compelling, and the two hues blend perfectly together to create a high-style traditional kitchen that is simply unforgettable.

USE DARK TONES TO REINFORCE TRADITIONAL STYLE. Darker woods and surface treatments are a hallmark of traditional kitchens, adding a somber feel and a more serious aspect. Here, brown countertops, stone tiles, and nearly-black cabinets create a bit of dark drama in the space. Tan walls and cutting-edge stainless steel appliances keep the look from becoming too dour or dim. When you need to counteract a dark space, bright shiny surfaces can be the perfect solution.

EMBELLISH A TRADITIONAL KITCHEN WITH FIXTURES. This decorative faucet has been crafted with a flowing shape indicative of traditional style, but it also has a darker "antique steel" finish that suits the style perfectly. A little searching will turn up a wealth of fixture options that blend perfectly with the traditional kitchen design you most fancy. Notice that this faucet also features handles rather than knobs, making it easier for children, the elderly, and anyone with dexterity issues to easily operate the faucet.

CHOOSE APPLIANCES TO BALANCE THE LOOK. Although many people think appliances should simply fade into the background, the beauty of modern appliances makes them perfect for display. Here, a stainless steel wall-mount oven counteracts the visually heavy feel of a dark run of cabinets, and a deep gray backsplash and countertop. The finish of the appliance actually blends with the finish of the cabinet pulls and handles, and the appearance is made more stunning with the use of the stainless steel front.

HANG COOKWARE TO DETAIL A TRADITIONAL KITCHEN. If your traditional kitchen is a little too sedate, you can spruce it up by bringing cookware out in the open. This is well in keeping with the parameters of a traditional design, and adds a lot of visual interest while also making it easier to access the cookware. You'll find hanging racks in a variety of materials, finishes, and designs.

INCORPORATE ORNATE FLOURISHES. The gorgeous, curvy chandeliers in this kitchen are the perfect complement to the detailed, luxury black-and-white cabinets. A pickled hardwood floor provides a neutral stage for a room design filled with drama, all without the aid of color. A wall of glass-fronted cabinets adds to the allure, as does the sophisticated choice of marble for the island countertop.

EXPLOIT CURVES AND FACADES. Flowing shapes and facings for common features such as refrigerators, other appliances, and the hood covering in this kitchen are hallmarks of traditional style. Notice how the façade over the range hood matches the finish and detailing on the cabinets throughout the space, and how the shape of the faucet mimics the window's arches. It's a design full of elegance in motion.

HIDE YOUR HOOD. Stainless steel doesn't fit comfortably into some traditional room designs and the answer is a hood overlay like the one shown here. It's an elegant solution where you want a somewhat warmer feel than cold steel. Both cabinet and appliance manufacturers are increasingly offering these kinds of overlays as luxury upgrades. You can find them to match just about any finish, or paintable so that you can customize to suit your particular design.

DETAILS SHOUT TRADITIONAL. Fluted columns, corbels, and frieze-ornamented cornices all make this a special kitchen and announce a traditional style. The visually stunning detailing of the cabinets and shelves is matched by their elegant muted green color. The fluted apron-front sink follows through on the theme, and the subway tile used for the backsplashes is the perfect decorative touch to contrast all the other flourishes in this room's design.

CAP THE DESIGN WITH CABINETS. Cabinetry is extremely important in defining a traditional style kitchen, and the cabinets usually set the tone for the rest of the decorative elements. But you can choose cabinets to accessorize as well, such as these beautiful units with glass-fronted top cabinets. The diamond muntins and tiered cornice scream high style without going over the top or outside the realm of what makes traditional traditional.

BRIGHTEN DARK, TRADITIONAL ROOMS. Use stainless steel to bring light to an overly dark kitchen by using the finish for all the appliances in the room. Stainless steel reflects even small amounts of light, creating the impression of a larger, airier space. It remains a sleek look for just about any kitchen and the right addition to a dark traditional space. In this case, because of all the dark, light-absorbent surfaces, the designer even included a stainless steel backsplash behind the range, adding the benefit of easy cleanup.

FINISH TO MATCH YOUR STYLE. Certain wood finishes are associated with the traditional kitchen style. These include the cherry finish shown here, mahogany stains, and dark walnut. Ebony stains, however, risk losing the fine details in cabinet profiles, columns, and corbels that are also so much a part of the traditional look. That's also why the finish is usually satin or semi-gloss for this style's cabinets.

MAKE MODERN INTRIGUING BY CONCEALING *AND* REVEALING. The open and hidden areas of storage in this modern kitchen provide a measure of visual intrigue in an otherwise spare space. Modern kitchens risk looking sterile, but having cookware and dishes on display adds warmth to the look. Not to mention, this strategy makes these items more accessible. The wood trim on the cabinets also adds a bit of relief in the largely monochromatic room.

GO FAUX FOR SAVINGS. Modern can be an expensive kitchen style to put in place, but you can get around some of the expense by using convincing and durable faux materials. Although this sleek, thick counter looks every bit as much stainless steel as the high-tech range hood, it is in fact, laminate. Modern laminates can be found mimicking all kinds of metals, stones, and even wood, and they are both durable and easy to work with.

ACCESSORIZE FOR MOD. Sleek sinks are a way to bring flair to a modern kitchen, and a round sink is unusual in any setting. This fashionable faucet-and-sink combo is a space-saving island addition and simple design feature that still brings a lot of visual impact. Sinks and faucets are fairly inexpensive ways to think out of the box and incorporate a slightly different look in your kitchen design.

DON'T FORGET THE HOOD STYLE. Cooktop hoods can often be afterthoughts in kitchen design, but a multi-feature, high-end hood such as the one shown here can accent a modern kitchen in fine style. This hood features multiple speeds, a digital readout, and integrated work lights, all in a cool linear package that would be at home in any modern setting. Hood manufacturers make many models to fit a modern setting.

SMALL DETAILS SPEAK LOUDLY IN MODERN DESIGN. Because modern kitchen design is defined by Spartan spaces, and clean, uncluttered lines and angles, little touches like the fine design handles shown here can play much larger than they normally would. There are a wealth of interesting handles and pulls on the market and it's easy to find a style that is both modern and to your taste.

GO BOLD. Although modern kitchen design is most often associated with bright white or neutral surfaces, you can bring your own signature to a modern kitchen with the judicious use of color. The kitchen here maintains a modern aesthetic with its sharp lines and angles and uncluttered décor. But it also leverages the power of color in the frameless cabinetry and the stunning recycled glass countertop. Both feature high-tech materials—another signature of modern style.

BRIGHT EQUALS MODERN. Much as modern is associated with clean, crisp lines, it's also defined by sharp, bright white lights. The halogens and LED fixtures used in this kitchen produce crisp white light perfect for a room that needs to be clean and easy to work in. Undercounter lights emphasize the stunning quartz countertops, while undercabinet lighting ensures that the surfaces are safe and easy to use.

CONSIDER A MODERN BLANK SLATE. Stay true to the uncluttered, linear perspective that defines modern style, and you can riff on it at the margins. Here, small points of color are captured in shelves and the drum shades of hanging light fixtures. The room is warmed up with wood tones and a simple band of glass tiles. A black range hood matches the black appliances used in the space and reinforces the modern aesthetic with a futuristic flair.

MATCH MODERN TO THE SPACE. A galley kitchen in a loft calls for an adapted modern design that better suits the space. The designer of this kitchen included the sharp stainless steel appliances you would expect, but incorporated subtly colored and textured cabinets that you wouldn't. The modern vibe is kept alive in the space with a white solid-surface countertop and a chrome X-leg dining table, but the look is as unique as it is modern.

THROW MODERN A CURVE. Modern kitchen designs are traditionally comprised of crisp lines and angles. But add a simple curve and you provide a bit of whimsy in an otherwise locked-down design style. This volcanic rock countertop not only supplies subtle but bright color, it also brings a little fun to the space, being shaped like a knife edge. It's a cool look for a room that is the definition of cool.

Modern

DEFY CONVENTION. The designer of this kitchen decided against wall-mounted cabinets, creating even more of an open feel to the room. The choice is inspired, because it reinforces the clean look that marks modern designs. That look is also helped by the rugged concrete countertops and the sophisticated— and super eco-friendly— marmoleum click flooring. The sum of the parts is a complete look that shouts "modern."

TILE A BACKSPLASH FOR VISUAL RELIEF. A tiled backsplash can have an effect far beyond its modest size. The cooktop backsplash in this small modern kitchen adds a whole lot of visual interest with the rectangular grid work and lovely blue color. The tile complements the other monochromatic and linear elements in the room, but also stands out as an elegant focal point in the spare, stylish space.

OPT FOR RAW IN INDUSTRIAL MODERN. This room is full of rough-hewn life with the plywood vertical island surfaces and concrete floors. The exposed edges of the countertop and shelves appears to be plywood as well, but is actually a sophisticated laminate surface, modern, edgy, and beautiful. The frosted-glass cabinet doors provide a simple, sophisticated, and subtle backdrop to what is a fairly dramatic modern island.

Country, Farmhouse & Cottage

COLOR COUNTRY KITCHENS IN CLASSIC TONES. The yellow here is right out of history and creates the perfect backdrop for stunning blue counters, antique-reproduction ceiling fixtures, and a fireclay farmhouse apron-front sink. The cabinets come equipped with detailing to match the historic paint and help create a beautiful and memorable kitchen design that is pure old-timey charm.

TAKE COUNTRY FROM ARCHITECTURAL CUES. The A-frame, exposed beam-and-rafter construction of this kitchen is reminiscent of a barn or farmhouse, so the designer filled the oversized space with country kitchen design elements, such as the simple recessed panel cabinets, wicker basket storage, and hanging fixtures that are reminiscent of candle lanterns. Decorative dinnerware on display adds to the effect. Country kitchen design is often thought of as a small room aesthetic, but here it works on a grand scale.

BRING FARMHOUSE STYLE TO LIFE WITH SUBTLY DETAILED CABINETRY. Although the cabinets in this kitchen look simple, the detailing is actually a thoughtfully accurate updated representation of authentic farmhouse cabinets. The recessed panels are true to the style, and arching kick plates create faux legs as if the cabinets were freestanding. Beautifully simple handles drive the impression home, and a copper range hood with decorative relief is the icing on the cake.

SET THE STYLE WITH THE SINK. No sink is quite so distinctive as an apron-front "farmhouse" sink. Named for the formidable cast iron fixtures that served as gigantic cleaning repositories for real farmhouses, this style of sink is beautiful and extremely useful because it is normally extremely deep. This particular version features an elegant tiered ledge and a stunning chrome faucet with white porcelain handles in keeping with the style of the sink. An incorporated soap holder makes the faucet even more useful.

SURROUND MODERN APPLIANCES WITH AN ANTIQUE LOOK. Upscale appliances such as the range and hood, refrigerator, and wall stoves in this kitchen are almost a necessity these days. To successfully incorporate these modern conveniences into the aged aesthetic of a country kitchen, surround them with key elements like these cabinets with vivid grain detail and simple butt-joint rail-and-stile construction. The juxtaposition creates visual interest, and the greater surface area of the cabinets ensures that the theme of the kitchen design predominates.

COUNTRIFY SMALL DETAILS. The ring of truth in any distinctive style is often established with the small convincing details. This chunky latch serves in place of a standard handle and catch, and provides a realistic antique farmhouse look to the cabinets. Hooded pulls in an antique finish could do the same. Details like this can make or break a stylized kitchen design.

USE WOOD TO ANNOUNCE FARMHOUSE STYLE. The wonderfully chunky wood island shown here, with its thick turned columns and matching wood-trimmed pot rack, sets the stage for the kitchen. The other cabinets follow suit, featuring a distressed finish, dish drying rack, and niche shelves—all indicators of country farmhouse style and all quaint design elements that create a lovely atmosphere in this kitchen. Keep in mind that the style is most closely associated with pine and oak, so if you're going to show a natural-finish wood surface in the space, best to use those.

CREATE A TUSCAN COUNTRY LOOK WITH STONE. The luxurious stone floor and diamond-pattern stone wall behind the range in this kitchen not only warm up the room, they also give it the feel of Italian countryside villa. These surfaces are indestructible and easy to clean as well. Antique reproduction ceiling pendants add to the feel, and a marble-topped wood island emphasizes the idea of lasting luxury. A chef-quality two-stove range with industrial hood fits right in with the rest of the design elements, mimicking the squat good looks of a wood-fired stove you might have found in an actual large Italian country house.

INDICATE COUNTRY STYLE WITH BEADBOARD. A design element that most definitely establishes old-fashioned kitchen design right out of a farm is a beadboard surface. The cabinets in this lovely, warm kitchen show the simple appeal of beadboard. They also boast antique-style pulls and handles, along with faux feet that really establish the impression of country style. Exposed beams drive the style home, as does the knotty pine flooring.

STORE IN PLAIN SIGHT IN A COUNTRY KITCHEN. The informal nature of country, farmhouse, or cottage-style kitchens means cookware, plates, glasses, and more are kept out on display. Open shelving often replaces cabinetry, and pot racks—like the handsome, rough-hewn version here—are a regular feature in the style. Set over the island, this rack not only adds a lot of visual interest, it also puts pots and pans right where they are needed.

GET FUNKY WITH COUNTRY. A country look lends itself to a little freestyle riffing on the theme. The designer here created the foundation of a country kitchen with the simple cabinets and diamond-pattern stone floor. But a leaded glass window, subway tile wall, and detailed cornice over the refrigerator all embellish the look with slight departures from the theme. Luxury stainless steel appliances provide visual focal points around the room and help guide the eye through the design.

SPECIAL SECTION:
Color in the Kitchen

White remains the most popular hue for kitchens. But that doesn't mean you have to jump on the colorless bandwagon. There are lots of color options for the kitchen, from bold to subtle. Even if you don't fancy coloring your kitchen top to bottom, you can inject splashes of color just about anywhere. Add a little blue in your backsplash, a bit of green on the front of your next stove, or choose cabinetry in a subtle yellow for a more widespread approach.

Using color in any kitchen design means seeing beyond trends. While bold colors were all the rage a few years ago, toned-down versions have become more popular recently. That doesn't mean you shouldn't use a bold color. It just means you need to make the choice wisely, so that the color ages as gracefully as the rest of your kitchen does.

The trick is picking colors you and your family can live with. Where bold colors are concerned—or those that you're on the fence about—it's wisest to use them in small, replaceable areas to begin with. A small island countertop, an isolated column of cabinets or a tiny backsplash are all prime spots for taking a chance on color. In other cases, you'll be more comfortable committing to the color. Where cabinets are colored in a traditional hue, such as the yellow cream perennially used in country kitchens, you can make the leap with the

BE FEARLESSLY BOLD WHEN YOU'RE SURE. If you absolutely love certain colors and you plan on owning your home for a good long time (if not the rest of your life), then don't be afraid to take the plunge and color the space to suit your preferences. This kitchen reflects just such a bold decision, indulging the homeowner's love of neon colors. The space is vibrant, high-energy, and happy. The color scheme is actually a coordinated complementary scheme with an analogous addition (the orange). It may not be for everyone, but it adds life and excitement to what might otherwise be a sedate space.

COMPLEMENT COLOR WITH DISTINCTIVE SINK FINISHES. Manufacturers now offer sinks in different finishes, shades, and colors, including the exceptional matte black shown here. In this case, the sink becomes the perfect natural color complement to a muted yellow countertop. An elegant arching chrome faucet with an easy-to-use handle and pull-down spray head makes this colorful picture as useful as it is visually delightful.

CONTAIN COLOR WITH MATCHING FIXTURES. Ensuring that fixtures throughout the space are finished in the same material and sheen gives the eye places to pause when it's processing strong color. Here, a brushed stainless steel sink and elegant matching faucet moderate the effect of a bold red countertop. A white sink would have worked as well, but it would have been less easy to match it to a high-style white faucet. The sink's apron front is an unusual design element that adds shape to a colorful visual and holds its own against the fiery backdrop of the counter.

confidence that the color is time-tested. Lighter or more subdued shades are also less likely to overwhelm the design or age too quickly in the space.

Select the right color and you'll be adding immeasurably to your kitchen design. Colors can warm or cool a space, they can make it livelier or create a calm sanctuary, and the right color can even make you happy every time you step into the room. So gather your paint chips, sample tiles, and other product swatches, and get thinking about color in your kitchen.

COMBINE COLOR AND TEXTURE FOR BIG, BIG BANG. The only thing better than a truly sophisticated mid-range blue tile is if that color sits underneath a randomly undulating surface. A backsplash or wall of tile like this can transform the kitchen, inviting the hands as well as the eyes, and creating a vivid focal point in the room. Use glass tile like this, and you'll also be incorporating an easy-to-clean surface that won't break the bank.

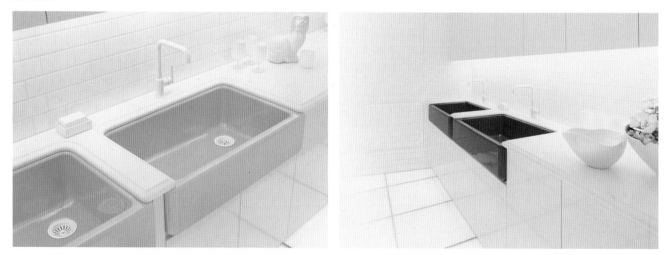

PUT A COLOR SPIN ON A CLASSIC. The simple apron-front sink is a truly timeless look that crosses the bounds of any specific kitchen design style. You can reinterpret this classic in an incredibly interesting way by using a colored version. As the samples here show, you can find all kinds of unusual colors in apron-front sinks. Find a hue you absolutely love, and the sink may just be the place to start with your kitchen redesign.

PARTNER PATTERN AND COLOR. Whether it's an exotic form of marble, wildly painted tile, or a recycled glass countertop like the one shown here, pattern is a natural companion to color, especially bold color. The color shows the variations in shapes and lines to its best advantage. A countertop like this can be a fairly risk-free way to introduce strong color into a kitchen, because if you limit it to one run of base cabinets, it can easily and inexpensively be replaced if you find the color is not exactly the one for you.

THINK BEYOND STAINLESS STEEL FOR YOUR HIGH-END APPLIANCES. Several manufacturers have joined the color parade with limited palettes of elegant colors to front their ranges, fridges, ovens, and other appliances. The four examples shown here represent the lovely range of offerings. Because these are fairly expensive appliances, you should choose a color carefully. But find the right one, and it can be the focal center point of your kitchen. The manufacturers have also taken pains to ensure the painted surface is every bit as cleanable and durable as stainless steel is.

CHILL WITH COLORS IN AN UNEXPECTED PLACE. Tinted refrigerators are a fairly new addition to the kitchen lineup, but one that can be a showstopper when used correctly. Some manufacturers offer completely colored versions, such as the incredibly fun and unusual jewel-toned units shown here. Others simply offer front panels that can be swapped in and out, to give the refrigerator a different look at different times. These are better used in traditional settings where the refrigerator is nested in a cavity and the sides don't show.

PLAY IT SAFE BY COLORING WITH TRADITION. Certain classic colors are inextricably linked to a certain design style. Using these hues in the style for which they were intended is an easy way to liven up a space with color. The dusty cornflower blue used in this country kitchen is the ideal marriage of simple form and lines with a color that's completely associated with that particular style. A muted cream yellow would have been just as appropriate, and just as timeless.

SYNC YOUR SINK COLORS. One of the marvelous modern innovations among today's manufacturers is coordinated sink-and-faucet color sets. A neutral tone such as the light brown sugar color of this sink and faucet are a safe choice, but one that will still draw a lot of attention in the kitchen. Although you can choose one of these sets in a color that contrasts the countertop, a more timeless look is a complementary pairing like the one shown here.

BRING CALM WITH GREEN. Mid-range and lighter greens are associated with nature, being the color of grass, leaves, and seedlings. Not surprising then that using splashes of green in the kitchen can create a feeling of calm in what can be a very hectic space. The secret is to stay away from overly bright greens that can seem a little too "neon" when covering a surface. This backsplash is an example of lovely and subtle mid-range green, one that won't grow tired over time.

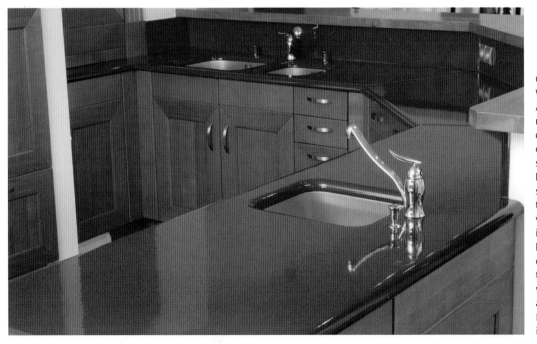

CONSIDER THE MATERIAL WHEN CONSIDERING A COLOR. Colors can read very differently on different materials. A fire-engine red like the one shown here could quickly look old if used on a matte surface in a kitchen. But as the coloring in a polished volcanic rock countertop, it brightens and comes to life. The surface treatment of this counter means that the color has incredible visual depth and richness, almost as if lit from within. If you love bold color, this is a great surface for it.

CREATE COLOR SURPRISES. A root beer brown sink that matches the finishes on base cabinets is a brilliant addition to this kitchen. Part of the charm is that the sink is concealed from view from many points in the kitchen. Only when the viewer approaches it, does its color become revealed. This use of color in the kitchen can be intriguing, engaging, and incredibly effective as a decorative device. The stylish chrome faucet adds a bit of brightness to the sink and complements it perfectly.

SEEK OUT UNUSUAL COLOR APPLICATIONS. The edge profiles of these paper-based fiber composite countertops come in different color combinations. It's a small color element but interesting and eye-catching. It doesn't hurt that these countertops are eco-friendly recycled paper—incredibly durable and easy to work with.

ESCHEW GLOSS FOR A DIFFERENT LOOK. Kitchen color doesn't have to be glossy to be beautiful. It's easy to fall into the trap of thinking all color surfaces in the kitchen must be shiny color surfaces. A gloss surface can sometimes make the color underneath seem a bit garish, or visually read too bright. The backsplash here shows what can be achieved with a more understated matte or satin surface. Even though these are glass tiles, you wouldn't know it from the sophisticated complementary colors under a non-reflective surface. Fortunately, the tiles are just as easy to clean as their high-gloss cousins.

LOOK TO THE FLOOR FOR COLOR CONTROL. A floor like the one in this country kitchen can be a perfect place for color, because you can control the exposure with the use of rugs and by moving furniture around. When using color in flooring, however, make sure the flooring is durable and cleanable, because otherwise the color could wind up looking dingy and actually make an unattractive surface more apparent. The marmoleum click surface used for this floor was ideal, because it's environmentally friendly, anti-bacterial, durable, easy to install, and competitively priced. You'll find marmoleum tiles in a range of beautiful colors.

CONFINE COLORS TO COUNTERTOPS TO KEEP FROM OVERWHELMING THE SPACE. The light green of the countertops used in this modern kitchen gives the space a fresh feel and makes it appear less sterile than it would if it had been kept all white. However, limiting the color to the countertops balances the visual weight in the space and ensures that it still holds true to a modern design aesthetic.

Spectacular Surfaces

Surfaces such as countertops and backsplashes play a big role in determining the look and style of any kitchen. Reflective surface materials can amplify available light in the room, add scintillating texture and pattern, and provide sturdy work surfaces that make food prep a pleasure. Matte surfaces absorb light, preventing visual "hot spots" or glare, and hide dirt well. Below the surface finish, you can choose from patterns, solids, and subtle variations. There are a lot of options, which make surface selection a fun and exciting part of the design process.

Start underfoot. Flooring sets the stage for other surfaces. It can be used as a focal point itself or merely as a backdrop for other decorative elements. It also provides the ever-important "feel" underfoot that can make a kitchen comfortable and pleasant. The look of the flooring has to work with the appearance of the other surfaces in the room. Beyond aesthetics, kitchen flooring must also be easy to clean and durable because the room is generally one of the busiest in any home.

Countertops are your chance to really make a statement in the space. Today's selection of countertop materials continues to grow with new synthetic variations and recycled materials of all kinds finding their way into countertop surfaces. All these different materials make for vastly different looks—one of which is sure to pique your interest.

MATCH NATURAL TO NATURAL. The stunning marble countertops in this kitchen work perfectly with the elegant, high-end wood cabinetry and oak flooring. From the stainless steel sink to the wood breakfast bar stools, the room is comprised of natural materials that are welcoming to the touch as well as the eye. Notice that the mid-range tones of the cabinets complements the marble and the other fixtures in the room. It's an entirely coordinated look that works on many levels.

GO DEEP FOR DRAMA. A thick countertop makes for an impressive appearance, as evidenced by this quartz surface. Quartz countertops can be manufactured in a variety of thicknesses and can include custom elements like the special long, skinny sink in this island. The look is slick and contemporary. However, thicker countertops are usually limited to islands, because base cabinet heights around the perimeter of the room restrict countertop thickness.

Natural materials like wood, glass, and metal all have their charm, and modern manufactured surfaces like vinyl and laminates are produced in an astounding array of appearances—some mimicking the look of natural materials, while others are purely unique. Among these many choices, you can select from those that are extremely eco-friendly, to other options that are far less so. Price will also have an effect on the choices you make, because the cost of different materials varies wildly.

Start with a look you like. Are you attracted to the warmth of wood counters or the clean professional appeal of stainless steel surfaces? Do you live in a hot climate where stone floors would make sense, or is your local weather better suited to warm, cushy linoleum underfoot? Do you expect to live in your current house for the foreseeable future (in which case, the cost of a high-end material such as marble or granite could be amortized over the long run)? Or do you see yourself moving on or trading up in a few years (making laminate countertops and floors the wiser choice)?

Consider the wealth of options in the pages that follow, and select the appearances that appeal most to you and the materials that will serve your purposes best. Just keep in mind as you consider the many possibilities that surfaces usually encompass the largest physical area in your kitchen, and therefore have a tremendous impact on the overall look and feel of the space.

STYLIZE SEDATE WITH A SOLID-COLOR SURFACE. One of the key decisions in choosing a countertop will be whether to choose patterns or a solid color. Although there are many intriguing patterned countertop materials, a solid color offers a clean, sleek, refined, and low-key appearance that is ideal for a contemporary kitchen such as this one. The gray quartz countertop here is super durable, and a beveled edge profile like the one on this counter gives it a nice understated detail.

Captivating Countertops & Backsplashes

USE QUARTZ TO DRESS UP A MODERN KITCHEN. White is the typical color for a modern kitchen, but you can add a bit of visual interest to an otherwise stark white room with an elegantly patterned quartz countertop. The wraparound island countertop shown here is all about sharp edges, a sleek surface, and sophisticated "barely there" mottling. It teases the eye and provides a bit of relief from the other bright white surfaces. It's also a tough surface that can withstand all kinds of food prep and any other abuse you can throw at it.

COLOR WITH QUARTZ. The method used to manufacture quartz solid-surface countertops allows manufacturers to color the surfaces with vivid hues. If you're after a showstopping appearance in your kitchen (especially if it's a modern space such as the one shown here), you might want to consider incorporating a boldly colored quartz countertop. Because they are nearly impossible to scar, the countertop will maintain its pristine and pure color for years, if not decades, to come.

ACCOMMODATE MULTIPLE OPENINGS IN A SINGLE SURFACE WITH QUARTZ. Because a quartz countertop can be fabricated to just about any specifications, you can design a countertop to contain double sinks, a cooktop, and more. This long surface keeps all the fixtures in order and looks sharp doing it. It also provides a surface that will hold up well to high traffic and lots of use and will be easy to clean at the end of the day—an extremely important feature if you're opting for an all-white counter!

UNIFY THE KITCHEN DESIGN WITH COUNTERTOPS. Different areas of this kitchen—oversized island, alcove oven area, and the sink—are visually tied together with the use of a stylish quartz countertop material. Although it looks like marble, this material is fabricated to suit the space—no mining necessary. It's also a great choice for multiple areas where different tasks will be performed; from the waterlogged area around the sink to the food prep done on the island, the material will hold up.

GO VERTICAL IN STYLE WITH QUARTZ. As much as it makes for a great countertop, a quartz slab can also serve as an easy-to-clean backsplash. The cooktop area shown here is kept neat and trim with a flat induction unit centered in a quartz countertop, with matching backsplash. It's a sleek look that can be executed easily wherever a quartz countertop butts up against a wall. It's also pretty simple to install.

BLEND COUNTERTOPS FOR A SEAMLESS LOOK. Mottled brown laminate countertops bring a lovely lighter look to this dark-toned kitchen, but the color blends perfectly with the other browns in the room. It's a stately appearance and, given the ample spaces the countertop must cover, a laminate surface was a wise choice. The material is relatively inexpensive, a fact belied by its handsome appearance.

STREAMLINE BY MATCHING SINK TO COUNTER. Here, a black laminate countertop is perfectly complemented with a glossy black sink and chic gooseneck faucet with valve handle and sprayer sharing a single deckplate. The faucet provides the sparkle, while the sink and counter create a dramatic black statement. Today's sinks come in a wide range of colors and finishes, so you should have no trouble matching yours to the countertop you want.

BUY STONE WITHOUT PAYING FOR STONE. Modern laminate counters offer incredible representations of other materials. The faux granite surface here is not just a repeating pattern as was used in the past. The manufacturer has gone to great pains to re-create the unique graining variations in an actual slab of granite. The result is a look that would be hard to discern from actual granite unless you were the homeowner or installer. Choose a laminate like this—and order an ogee edge profile like the one shown here—and you'll have all the beauty of a real granite surface at a fraction of the cost.

PICK A MATTE FINISH FOR AN ALWAYS-SHARP LOOK. This may look like slate, but it's actually a laminate, low-luster surface that gives the counter a very sophisticated appearance. It also makes it easy to see and clean up spills, and far less likely to show any signs of wear, tear, or aging. All in all, a matte surface texture has a lot going for it and is worth some consideration in your search for the ideal countertop.

FIND THE UNUSUAL—AND SPECTACULAR—AMONG MODERN LAMINATES. Today's laminate countertops come in an astounding diversity of patterns and colors that gives you the means to affect just about any look you might want in your kitchen for a very reasonable cost. This laminate countertop is on the wild side of the spectrum, featuring the stunning appearance of petrified wood in a thick profile that makes the counter look like one gigantic slab of old-growth forest. It's unique, well suited to the cabinets and space, and tremendously eye-catching.

Captivating Countertops & Backsplashes

LET LAMINATE REPRODUCTIONS TAKE YOU WHERE THE ACTUAL MATERIALS CAN'T GO. A 12-foot long butcher block counter would be an incredibly difficult surface to fabricate even if you were willing and able to foot the bill or craft it yourself. But make that countertop out of a faux-butcher block laminate and you've achieved the look you wanted with less expense and hassle. This beautiful countertop is almost indistinguishable from the real thing, and fits right into the look of this industrial loft kitchen.

SPEND LESS FOR QUARRY STONE. Few looks say luxury like the appearance of a marble surface in a well-appointed kitchen. You'd be hard-pressed to find anyone who didn't recognize these counters as marble, and the look is undeniably posh. But it's also undeniably affordable. The surfaces are all extremely convincing reproductions of marble surfaces. It's a surefire look that really makes the kitchen shine. Reproducing the appearance of high-end quarry stone is one of the things modern laminates do best—and it's a great way to have the look and impression of marble with a much lower cost.

HIDE THE SEAM. Modern laminate manufacturers have developed a lot of ways to conceal edge seams—the primary giveaway that the counter is actually a laminate and not a stone surface. The illusion is kept complete with this countertop through the use of a bullnose front edge. This is only one of many edge profiles laminate countertop suppliers can create, but all are designed to minimize any seams so that the counter seems to be something it is not.

GO WILD WITH LAMINATES. Want a truly unusual, unique, and exceptional countertop look? You might not think that laminates can deliver—but those were your mother's laminates. These days, laminate countertops come in truly inventive designs, like this one with a dotscreen pattern on top and a banded wood "plywood" pattern on the drop front. The design confuses the eye and creates a riveting visual that could easily be the focal point of your kitchen. This is just one of the many surprising surface designs offered in laminate countertops today—there's likely one just perfect for any kitchen design you have in mind.

Captivating Countertops & Backsplashes

GET GRANITE FOR GORGEOUS LOOKS. Granite is the most popular quarry stone used for countertops in the home and for good reason. It comes in a range of colors and surface patterns, each more elegant than the last. With minimal maintenance, the countertop will last just about forever and it can endure heat, knife blades, and all manner of abuse without looking timeworn. These particular countertops are actually granite shells, made of pieces leftover from the fabrication of solid granite surfaces. Although they are less expensive than a solid surface, they are every bit as durable and beautiful—and available in every color and pattern granite offers.

MARRY GRANITE TO OTHER RAW, NATURAL MATERIALS. This speckled granite countertop could not seem more at home than it is paired with natural-finish wood cabinets that allow the vivid graining to show through and a solid steel pot rack that brings stainless steel cookware out in the open. All the surfaces seem to reinforce the idea that this is a cook's kitchen. The granite puts an elegant icing on an earthy, handsome design.

ENLARGE WITH GRANITE. Granite, like other luxury surface materials, is perfect for small spaces, bringing a touch of luxury for far less than it would cost to outfit a larger kitchen. The black granite used here provides a dramatic counterpoint to the largely white room—a color choice that was meant to keep the small kitchen visually large. The elegance of the countertops is well matched to the glass-front cabinets and high-end light fixture.

MAKE IT SPECIAL WITH MARBLE. Although this craftsman style country kitchen has a lovely understated appeal with its cream yellow color and true-to-form cabinetry, the marble countertops put the design over the top. The white-and-green veined marble is perfect for the space, and because the kitchen is fairly modest in size, splurging on marble countertop surfaces didn't break the bank for the homeowner. This kitchen proves that the right marble surfaces in the right place provides a lot more design bang for whatever bucks you might have spent.

Captivating Countertops & Backsplashes

MATCH A TABLE FOR A COORDINATED LOOK. The stunning, stainless steel-topped dining table in this kitchen sets the tone for the countertops. Stainless steel was an insightful choice because it carries through the theme of a high-end, serious cooking area anchored by the restaurant quality range. The countertops are easy to clean and a sleek accent to the frameless European-style cabinets and designer pendant lighting.

BRIGHTEN SMALL SPACES WITH STAINLESS STEEL SURFACES. This tiny kitchen is kept visually open with the use of light-colored frameless cabinetry and stainless steel counters, backsplashes, and appliances. The metal surfaces reflect a maximum of light and provide a clean, uncluttered appearance. They are also easy to clean, which can be a crucial factor in small busy kitchens.

LET STAINLESS STEEL DOMINATE. Clad a large island like this entirely in stainless steel and the result is a clean, inviting kitchen design. Complement the stainless steel with white walls and ceilings, and incorporate a complementary flooring such as this stunning, light-colored surface. This floor looks like wood, but it's not. It's actually incredibly detailed glazed porcelain tile—a feature that adds immeasurably to the chic look of this kitchen.

CAPTURE VISUAL INTEREST WITH COPPER. Copper is as well suited to kitchen countertops as other metals, but is used much more rarely because it can be more expensive and cladding surfaces in the metal often requires particular expertise. But order a custom counter and backsplash like this one, and the effort and expense can quickly seem worth it. Keep in mind that copper is a distinctive look, one that works with a limited number of cabinet styles. The custom cabinets shown here are ideal for the eclectic nature of this kitchen design. Copper is often best used "distressed" as it has been in this kitchen, which gives it an authentic, warm, and interesting appearance.

CONFUSE THE EYE WITH ZINC. This may look like stainless steel, but it is actually polished zinc. Zinc has been used for the countertops in European bars for over a century, but it also makes a great kitchen countertop material. The installer can seal the surface of the zinc to protect it, but you might be wiser to let the natural zinc surface be. It can be affected by skin oils, lemon juice, and other materials, giving the surface a patina and marks that many people feel are its most alluring traits. It's on par with the cost of a stainless steel surface, but much more distinctive.

INTRODUCE BOLD ACCENTS WITH GLASS COUNTERTOPS. Because these countertops are produced using glass from a variety of sources, they come in almost every color of the rainbow, including vivid hues like the blue of this surface. You don't need to commit to the color throughout the space; you can incorporate the material as a small section of countertop like a work surface next to the cooktop, as shown here. One of the advantages of this type of countertop is that it can be fabricated to nearly any shape, such as the partial dogleg at the back edge of this counter.

COMPLEMENT OTHER COUNTERTOPS WITH RECYCLED GLASS. The busy patterns of a recycled glass surface can overwhelm a kitchen with several large expanses of countertop. But use the material in one area of the kitchen—like the breakfast bar L in this room—and you create a dynamic accent that adds life to an otherwise subtle kitchen design. Notice that the designer selected a recycled glass surface in muted grays, a choice that dials back the visual power of the material and blends it more seamlessly with the other solid-color countertops.

OPT FOR RECYCLED GLASS COUNTERS FOR MAXIMUM PATTERN AND COLOR. Although dynamic color is the most obvious selling point for recycled glass countertops, these surfaces also provide the opportunity to introduce mesmerizing patterns into the kitchen. Choose the color carefully as this homeowner did, so that the hues blend naturally with other tones in the room—the dominant brown in this countertop complements the cabinet below. Get the color right, and the pattern becomes a riveting design element. This countertop illustrates the intense interest that can be created by large and small pieces of glass randomly intermingled.

Captivating Countertops & Backsplashes

HAVE FUN WITH RECYCLED GLASS. Because they can be blended with just about any mix of colors, you can create a jubilant, smile-making kitchen design around the right recycled glass surface. This L-shaped counter combines a mix of carnival colors that are moderated by the white substrate. It's an incredibly fun look, but not so busy that it's overwhelming. If your kitchen design is a little eclectic and you're willing to take the plunge into whimsy, this could be the perfect countertop choice.

MATCH GLASS WITH GLASS. A recycled glass countertop is a natural choice to pair with other glass design elements in the kitchen. The surface here was selected in a color that blends with the colors of the glass tile backsplash, the green glass inserts in the upper cabinets, and the appliance front panel. The wealth of reflective surfaces make this small space seem bright and airy, and the countertop and backsplash ensure that it is also easy to keep clean.

EXPLORE NEW TECHNOLOGY FOR STUNNING COUNTERTOPS. This cutting edge fused-glass surface is created with a combination of new and recycled glasses, creating an unusual and exciting appearance. Manufacturers continue to explore new horizons with existing materials to create spectacular countertop surfaces like this. Expand your search if what you're after is a design focal point surface for your kitchen.

COUNT ON RECYCLED GLASS FOR DURABILITY. The fabrication process used to create these surfaces makes them stable and tough. The counters can withstand knife blades, hot pots, and other abuse every bit as well as a granite countertop can. It's even stable enough to stand up to a cantilevered installation like the combination island and breakfast bar in this kitchen. Take your time in choosing from among the many color options, because the countertop is sure to have a long, long life.

COMBINE GLASS WITH OTHER MATERIALS FOR SHOWSTOPPING COUNTERS. There are many ways to incorporate glass surfaces into kitchen countertops. Although the most common are complete countertops and recycled glass, many companies offer custom fabrication services to create one-of-a-kind installations like the cast glass oval countertop shown here. The surface has been incorporated into an engineered concrete countertop, creating an attention-getting feature in an otherwise understated kitchen.

COLOR YOUR KITCHEN SOPHISTICATED WITH VOLCANIC ROCK. These countertops come in 16 glossy and 16 matte colors, ranging from magnificent reds to the chic elegance of the blue shown here. The colors are fired onto the volcanic rock surface, creating an alluring visual depth that is unique among countertop materials. Although the bolder colors are usually used sparingly, the more understated shades like this can transform a kitchen and serve as countertops throughout even a large room.

OUTFIT HIGH-USE AREAS WITH DURABLE VOLCANIC ROCK. This countertop material really comes into its own in prep and cooking areas. The enamel glaze that colors the surface is fired onto the rock at temperatures around 1000°F, so it's nearly indestructible. It will hold up to knives, hot pots, and even bleach cleansers without a mar or a stain. A high-use location, such as the island prep surface next to a cooktop in this kitchen, is the perfect opportunity to let this material shine.

INCORPORATE NIFTY BUILT-IN EXTRAS WITH VOLCANIC ROCK COUNTERS. The fabrication process used to create these countertops allows for special features to be crafted right into the structure of the countertop. This bright white sink counter is evidence of what can be done with the material; a stepped-down sink section was made with integrated drainboards on either side of the sink. The finished edge allowed for an undermount sink, and custom holes accommodate a high-end faucet with independent handles.

Captivating Countertops
& Backsplashes

PAIR DISTINCTIVE SINKS WITH DISTINCTIVE COUNTERS. A wide plank wood countertop, finished in stunning ebony, is perfectly accented with a hammered undermount copper sink. It's a masterful pairing of finishes that each amplify the visual effect of the other. This is an example of making a wood countertop even lovelier than it might have been if finished natural.

MAKE THE MOST OF WOOD EDGE GRAIN DETAIL. This walnut countertop not only makes great use of a classic and beautiful hardwood, but the countertop is comprised of end grain pieces, which are the hardest and most durable to cut. The end grain creates exceptional patterns that beg to be finished naturally, as has been done on this countertop. Use a satin finish to avoid distracting glare hot spots and create a truly sophisticated look.

EXPLOIT WOOD'S DECORATIVE POTENTIAL. Want the beauty of a wood countertop like the wide plank teak surface in this kitchen? Don't forget the details. This countertop includes a detailed edge molding around the inside of an undermount sink. Creating a look like this means painstakingly finishing the wood to ensure that the counter and molding are not damaged by water, and sealing the sink seam to prevent any leaks. But the results are well worth the effort, as this example clearly shows.

GO BEYOND BUTCHER BLOCK FOR INCREDIBLE STYLE. Wood plank counters are a step up from the common and folksy butcher block. Not only do hardwoods offer fascinating intricate grain patterns, they are also prime candidates for custom cutting and fabrication into ornate shapes like the island countertop in this kitchen. The outline of the counter echoes the shape of the base legs, and presents an incredible edge profile that helps boost the stately cred of the entire kitchen design. A dark brown finish was an inspired choice and, although the wood should not be used as a cutting surface, it is resistant to other abuse and moisture.

Captivating Countertops & Backsplashes

GO ECO-FRIENDLY AND HEALTHY. This satiny surface may look like slate, but it's actually a recycled paper countertop. Made from 100 percent post-consumer waste combined with natural binders and pigments, the surface is remarkably durable. It won't stain, is not susceptible to moisture damage, and cuts or abrasions can be sanded out. It will also hold up to a lot of wear and tear. You'll find recycled paper countertops in a range of neutrals and earth tones, at prices competitive with other options. And the counters don't have a negative impact on indoor air quality, so you'll be doing your family—and the environment—a favor.

ADD SHARP, CLEAN LINES WITH RECYCLED PAPER SURFACES. Although the edges of this type of countertop can be fabricated with many different profiles (a carbide tip router is all it takes), the countertops come from the manufacturer with a sleek flat front. Use the plain edge in a kitchen like this one, with crisp lines defining the design, and bright white halogen lights highlighting the details in the surfaces. Keeping the original edge profile also makes installing the countertop a much easier project.

SHAPE TO SUIT. Because they are colored uniformly all the way through, recycled paper countertops can be cut to many different shapes. This curving tiered countertop is an example of what can be done with the material. The top counter surface is also a thicker-than-normal panel—the material is sold in different thickness. Choose based on the look you want. These properties make recycled paper countertops adaptable to a wide range of kitchen styles and personal design preferences.

PICK A FINISH THAT SUITS YOU. One of the wonderful things about a recycled paper countertop is that you can use the satin finish with which the material is manufactured, or use finishing products—available from the manufacturer—to create a high-gloss surface. Use it where you want to brighten the naturally toned-down color, or where you want to amplify the available light in the room. Note that these counters are also great for use with undermount sinks like the one shown here. Seal the edges and there will be no problems with moisture infiltration.

GET EDGY WITH RECYCLED PAPER SURFACES. Some recycled paper countertops are offered with special exposed edge treatments, like the sample shown here. Compressed layers are shown in cutaway edges, and add a delicate bit of visual interest to the side of the countertop. This edge treatment is available in different colors, all of which complement the top color, making it easy to coordinate the look in your kitchen. Details like these are a way to put your own signature on the kitchen design.

Captivating Countertops & Backsplashes

STAY INFORMAL WITH BUTCHER BLOCK. Traditional butcher block is warm and welcoming, unfussy and durable. Those qualities help it fit right into a Euro-style kitchen like this, complemented by a stainless steel sink and countertop, exposed hanging storage, and simple machined glass cabinet fronts. The design is all about open airiness and casual relaxation, and the butcher block surfaces help drive the theme home—not to mention making wonderful places for food prep.

SEPARATE YOUR ISLAND WITH A HANDY BUTCHER BLOCK TOP. Islands are some of the most common locations for butcher block countertops because they are usually centers of activities such as food prep as well as being visual centers of the room. A butcher block island counter makes the fixture eminently usable and warms up the room. This makes it a great surface for a room with stainless steel counters or any other countertop materials that are reflective and visually "cold."

MAKE SMALL-BACKSPLASH MAGIC WITH MOSAICS. The multi-colored dichroic glass tiles in this kitchen's cooktop backsplash add both iridescent color and minute pattern to the room. The busy small shapes play off the small squares and rectangles of stained glass in the finely detailed craftsman-style lighting fixtures. The dichroic mosaic tiles will appear to change colors at different viewing angles and under different lighting, making this a modest feature with lots of design power.

SAY "SERIOUS" WITH A STEEL BACKSPLASH. Stainless steel can serve as a startlingly unusual backsplash, one that sends the message that the kitchen is meant for cooking. A sumptuous quartz countertop adds to the impression, adding beautiful pattern under the crisp silver surface of the backsplash. Both countertop and backsplash are smart choices where cleanup is concerned, and both are extremely durable, so splashes and spills won't leave stains. The backsplash also ties the entire kitchen together, providing a visual link between the range and other appliances and the walls of the kitchen.

MAKE A SOPHISTICATED STATEMENT WITH A BACKSPLASH WALL. The green glass tiles behind this high-end electric induction range are manufactured with a color backing that gives the glass surface a uniform color. Using oversized tiles helps tie the wall design to the rest of the room, because the grid of lines mimics the clean, linear aspect of the cabinets in the space, as well as the shape of the other design elements such as the range hood. It's a super sleek, eye-catching appearance that was simple and easy to create.

SELECT SPECIALTY TREATMENTS FOR BACKSPLASHES.
The small coverage area of many backsplashes means
you won't break the bank if you opt for a high-end,
extremely unusual surface treatment. The homeowner
here selected an intricate woven metal panel that looks
like the side of a finely crafted wood basket. Not only is
this a riveting visual in its own right, but the pattern and
color help make the marble counter and stylish modern
faucet-and-sprayer combo really pop. It's a one-of-a-kind
look that is pure chic.

TILE FOR A TIMELESS LOOK. Ceramic and stone tile remain extremely popular backsplash options. One of the key reasons for this popularity is
the incredible diversity of surface appearances, from glossy to matte, to solid color and beyond. Simple stone tiles like those used in this country
kitchen are a classic look that lends a bit of visual interest behind the stove and counter. The tiles are easy to install, and the grout lines are less
prone to staining on the vertical surface than they would be on a counter or floor.

Captivating Countertops & Backsplashes

TIE A ROOM TOGETHER BY EXTENDING A BACKSPLASH TREATMENT. You can unify a kitchen design by covering entire walls with the same surface material you use for the backsplash. The black mosaic tile in this room would make a stunning backsplash, but used across two walls, it makes the red cabinetry pop and provides the perfect backdrop to luxury stainless steel appliances. It's also a lovely compliment to the smaller mosaic tile used on the floor. This is a very effective design technique, especially in smaller kitchens.

CREATE A BACKSPLASH ACCENT WALL. By using the entire wall as a backsplash, you increase the visual power of the feature—well worth considering when you're covering the surface with hip glass tiles like those shown here. The tiles used in this kitchen include a range of shapes and neutral hues, all of which complement the brown walls, cabinets, and countertops. It's a perfectly coordinated look, but one that puts the focus on the accent wall, proving that you can never go too big with a backsplash surface.

MAKE MOSAIC MAGIC. Don't settle for plain, ordinary mosaics on your backsplash. Look a little further and you'll find very special mosaic tiles (sometimes special order) that will create a simple stunning vertical surface. These tiles have a gold-leafed surface that shimmers in luxuriant tones and changes appearance under different lights. All its different tones blend perfectly with the elegant laminate countertop and brown cabinets. You can also choose from metal mosaics and upscale quarry stone versions.

REFINE THE LOOK WITH MONOCHROMATIC TILE. You can do a lot with a few simple shades of a neutral color, especially when you use tiles in different shapes, like the glass tiles covering this backsplash and wall. Some manufacturers make this easier than it looks, by joining the tiles on standardized sheets that are easy to install. But in any case, the subtle shadings supply just enough visual interest to add to the kitchen design without creating visual noise.

TEXTURE YOUR BACKSPLASH TO INVITE TOUCH AND COMPLIMENTS. A little added texture only heightens the look of a high-style backsplash like this. By interspersing textured tiles in shades of the same color, the homeowner creates endless fascination for the eye and a treat for the fingers (as long as the burners aren't lit). The trick is to either use all textured tiles, or use a mixture with colors that blend seamlessly. That way you'll impress your guests without overwhelming the eye.

MATCH UNUSUAL FLOORING TO AN UNUSUAL DESIGN. This spectacular kitchen features a quote relief along the wall-top molding, a map of London as a backsplash, and period-style lamps and drapes, all topped off with luxury, pro-quality stainless steel appliances. It's an eclectic but thoughtful design that is perfectly set off by a hexagonal mosaic tile floor. The floor's character seems right in keeping with all the other face-forward, distinctive design elements, and the white coloring ensures that the space is not overwhelmed with dark tones.

BE TIMELESS WITH STONE TILE. Flooring like the soapstone tiles in this kitchen will not only last the life of the kitchen, the look never goes out of style. Although you can opt for granite, marble, or ceramics if you're after pronounced color or patterns, soapstone is a great choice for an understated floor underfoot, one that features very subtle variations and a forgiving surface that is low maintenance. The look of sandstone also transcends design styles; this floor would be just as at home in a contemporary setting as it is in this Euro-country kitchen.

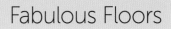

GLASSIFY YOUR FLOOR. Although they're widely popular as backsplashes, not many homeowners know the incredible flooring possibilities glass tiles offer. You can design an ornate floor pattern such as the one shown here—including larger rectangles with small squares—or just go with a more simple design of one solid color and one uniform size of tile. Either way, you'll find an incredible array of colors, sizes, and surface finishes from high gloss to the matte texture of this floor.

INTERSPERSE TILE TREATMENTS TO GUIDE THE EYE. The kitchen shown here features a classic herringbone stone tile floor with a modern skinny glass tile backsplash. The two looks are kept from competing by the clean contemporary cabinetry in the room. Using a feature with solid colors and clean lines to separate busier surfaces is a great way to incorporate different dynamic patterns into a kitchen while keeping them from overwhelming the space with visual busyness.

INTRODUCE LUXURY WITH A MARBLE TILE FLOOR. There's no getting around the beauty of a marble tile floor. It's a classically elegant look that is as high-style as you can get. Although it's one of the most expensive flooring materials, it's also going to last the life of the house and never go out of style. It's wise to pair the look with other upscale features, such as the sleek contemporary dishwasher shown here, with a custom front panel that blends seamlessly with the base cabinets in the room.

Fabulous Floors

SYNC SUBTLE WITH SIMPLE TILES. The very basic cream-colored ceramic tile in this kitchen is perfect for the low-key, neutral-colored design. It complements the light-hued frameless base cabinets and the off-white upper cabinets. It also creates the ideal stage to show off an upscale stainless steel gas range. Using neutral colors and minimal patterns and lines is a great way to showcase high-end appliances or special features in the kitchen.

REINFORCE RUSTIC STYLE WITH TRAVERTINE TILES. This particular stone tile is closely associated with Italian Tuscan style, as well as other continental country styles. It's both a sophisticated and old-world rural look that adds flavor to a country kitchen. Embellish a kitchen design like this with backsplash tiles that match the natural earth tones in the floor, such as the rectangular porcelain tiles used on the wall behind this sink. Add a few dozen bottles of wine for a particularly authentic look and dining pleasure.

MAKE YOUR KITCHEN HEALTHY WITH MARMOLEUM®. Marmoleum is the modern version of linoleum and comes in easy-to-install tiles called "click" flooring. The number of colors, patterns and looks available in marmoleum are incredible, and a simple color blend such as the yellow-and-white scheme in this country kitchen is just one of many possible combinations. Marmoleum, like linoleum, is anti-bacterial, doesn't off-gas any volatile compounds, and is made of natural ingredients, all of which makes it one of the greenest flooring materials you can choose.

Fabulous Floors

PICK VINYL FOR A CONVINCING FAUX SURFACE. This kitchen may look like it sports a stunning stone floor in a variety of tile sizes, but it's actually vinyl. Vinyl flooring is offered in a cornucopia of surface appearances and even in a variety of textures. Manufacturers offer versions of just about every quarry stone look you might consider, at a fraction of the cost of the real thing. And today's vinyl flooring is tough and easy to clean as well.

TAKE YOUR KITCHEN DESIGN IN A NEW DIRECTION. Vinyl tiles like these are easy to install and give you a chance to put your own imprint on your kitchen design. By mixing and matching tiles with the same coloration—and by mixing the direction of the "grain" in the tiles—you have endless options for making the look of your kitchen floor totally unique. No matter how it looks, you'll be saving money with a custom appearance.

COMBINE COMFORT WITH LUXURY. This modern space is perfectly outfitted with a beautiful slate floor . . . except that the floor is vinyl. Notice that even the texture is correct—it's almost impossible to tell it from actual stone. Well, until you walk across the floor and feel the cushion and warmth underfoot. Dropped glassware and dishes are also less likely to break on this version than they would on a true slate floor.

ENJOY THE WARMTH OF WOOD WITHOUT THE WORK. Wood kitchen floors are gorgeous and perfectly in keeping with the country kitchen style of this room. But save yourself the effort and expense by buying a vinyl version like the one shown here. It looks exactly like a wood floor, but is completely waterproof and far less expensive. What's more, it will never need to be sanded and refinished.

FOREGO SEAMS FOR A SMOOTH, APPEALING SURFACE. When you want your floor to play a supporting role in the drama of the kitchen design, a simple mono-color surface with no seams is just the ticket. Vinyl sheet like the floor in this kitchen answers the call in style. Vinyl sheet is often laid by professionals, but is also a completely achievable DIY project. Once installed, the flooring is waterproof, resistant to stains, dents, and scratches, and it won't fade over time.

FINESSE THE FLOOR WITH BORDERS. The elegant borders in this floor would be painstaking and expensive to achieve were the floor really stone tile. But because it's actually a reproduction in vinyl, the borders are easy and inexpensive to introduce into the design. Special features like this are no problem when you choose vinyl and can be mixed and matched to create a truly stunning floor in any kitchen.

Fabulous Floors

BAFFLE THE EYE WITH CORK. Cork floor tiles can be dyed a range of different colors and when colored solid so that the grain doesn't show through, the floor is almost impossible to identify. Cork takes stain extremely well, creating a visual depth that is warm and intriguing. A floor design like this is also essentially timeless, because it uses neutral tones that will work with dark or light cabinetry and a full range of other surfaces.

BE ENVIRONMENTALLY FRIENDLY WITH YOUR FLOOR. Cork is an entirely natural substance that is moisture resistant and easy to clean. Cork tiles like these are usually given a natural finish to allow the character of the material to really shine. There are many non-toxic sealants and finishing products for cork floors, which will help the floor last a good long time and look good for its entire life. All that, and a warm, super cushy surface underfoot account for the growing popularity of this intriguing flooring material.

DRAMATIZE YOUR KITCHEN. When carefully stained, cork tiles can take on the alluring appearance of timeworn stone. The floor here is a clear example of the deep, rich coloring that can be achieved by staining and finishing a cork floor with an aged appearance in mind. Cork floors are also a doable DIY project, even when you want to include a special feature like the border in this floor. All it takes is a little planning and bit of work, and you could have floor that mimics stone but feels like walking on a cloud.

Fabulous Floors

GET YOUR COUNTRY STYLE ON WITH WOOD FLOORING. A themed kitchen like this, with authentic recessed panel cabinets and antiqued pulls, latches, and hinges, calls for true wood floor. The dusty yellow of the cabinets is complemented perfectly by the light tones of the oak strip flooring. The floor seems almost like an extension of the wood-finished island, and it provides a visual stage for the beautifully colored cabinets.

RECLAIM A PIECE OF THE PAST. You can have a unique wood floor full of character and charm by using reclaimed wood strips or planks. Taken from older buildings being demolished or those that are just falling down, these materials contain imperfections, marks, and colorings that can't be found anywhere else and certainly not in new wood. A floor like the one in this country kitchen lends a sense of comfort and authenticity to the room and creates a look like no other.

LET WOOD SET A WARM TONE. This kitchen features a sharp, clean look with stunning white-trim cabinets and quartz countertops. Gloss white paint and a shiny countertop surface can lead the design to be somewhat cold, but the use of a handsome wood floor—along with a handy extendable wood cutting board—lends warmth and visual depth to the room and provides a comfortable surface underfoot. The surface slightly cushions impacts and can save the occasional dropped glass or plate.

COMBINE BASIC RAW MATERIALS FOR AN EARTHY NATURAL APPEAL. The wood strip flooring in this eclectic kitchen is the ideal complement to the exposed brick, steel ductwork, and recycled paper countertop. Like the matte surface of the countertop and the rough-hewn joints in the brickwork, the wood floor adds an inviting depth and warmth to the room. It's hard to go wrong with any combination of wood, metal, masonry, and other natural materials in a room where comforting meals are served.

Fabulous Floors

EXPLOIT WOOD STAINS FOR UNIQUE LOOKS. Wood floors certainly look handsome finished natural, but staining a wood surface an unusual shade is a great way to get even more design bang out of the flooring. The gray stain used on this kitchen floor provides the perfect stage for an upscale, reserved contemporary kitchen design, and the choice of satin—rather than gloss—stain is inspired. The floor contrasts the lighter cabinets and furniture in the space, creating a wonderful visual balance with just enough dynamic tension to keep things interesting.

DRESS UP A FLOOR WITH BORDERS AND INSETS. Although these features take a little planning to install correctly, a medallion, border, or other inset area, like the base border around the island in this kitchen, can be a real show-stopper. Whenever you use a border or other inlaid design, the point is to make it as pronounced as possible. That's why the homeowner decided on different woods and different finishes for the inlaid design in this floor. If you're going to the trouble and expense of installing a special flooring feature, flaunt it!

SAVE MONEY WITH LAMINATES. Have your eye set on a nice oak strip floor, like this one? Well, you need to adjust your eyes and prepare for thrift, because this is laminate flooring. Created with a photographic layer underneath a durable clear layer of plastic, laminates come in a range of surface appearances, but the most popular are wood. The look is convincing and installing the floor is a fairly easy weekend project for the moderately accomplished DIYer.

SELECT A LAMINATE FOR THE LONG HAUL. The incredible variety of surface appearances means you have lots of choices to select from when shopping for laminates. But in a basic contemporary kitchen like this, it's wise to choose a look—like the mid-range oak-strip-style laminate here—that will continue to work in your kitchen design as you change or update it. A floor like this is durable enough to last a decade and will work with cabinets, countertops, and walls from light to dark, traditional to modern.

Stylish Kitchen Storage

Storage is essential to the success of any kitchen design and determines how comfortable and efficient the kitchen will be. A lack of storage—or the wrong kind in the wrong place—will make a kitchen difficult to cook in and a less-than-pleasant place for socializing and relaxation. Fortunately, setting up the proper storage for how you want to use the kitchen is not difficult, given the many different options available. Shop wisely and you can take the opportunity to also enrich your kitchen design in wonderful ways.

The first and most important decision you'll need to make is between exposed or hidden storage. Look at what you need to store, and then assess the best way to store it. Some items, such as pots and pans, can be kept in a large cabinet or drawer, but also look great on display hanging from a rack. Other things, such as pantry dry goods like flour, cereal, and canned foods, are best kept concealed behind closed doors.

Regardless of what you need to store, start with the biggest storage first. That usually means cabinets. Cabinets are a big investment in time, money, or both, and are a major design element in any kitchen. No matter what cabinets you choose, exploit the many different organizing options among today's cabinet inserts. You'll find ideas to keep spices close at hand and ways to access large bulky pots or cooking aids more easily.

Supplement your cabinet space with shelving, racks, or even standalone units, and you'll soon have a kitchen that is wonderfully efficient, a pleasure to spend time in, and beautiful as well.

COORDINATE STORAGE. The stunning cabinets in this kitchen are complemented by matching shelves that hold cookbooks and other attractive kitchen items. The simple yet timeless style of the cabinets is carried through in island side panels that mimic the rail-and-stile cabinet doors. The light wood tones are echoed in the choice of table and chairs, and all the pieces together establish a very light, airy, and pleasant feeling in the room.

SIMPLIFY WITH BAMBOO. The eco-friendly bamboo cabinets shown here are typical, featuring uncomplicated lines in a frameless construction with understated graining. Bamboo is usually stained natural, although it takes colored stain well and can even be ebonized. You'll find slightly different grain patterns in different cabinets, but all are subtle and pretty. Best of all, the material is a grass, not actually a wood, so it grows fast and harvesting it is a sustainable practice.

EMPHASIZE GRAIN PATTERNS. Basic raised-panel cabinets like these can certainly be painted or stained very dark, but staining them light not only keeps a small kitchen like this one light and feeling expansive, it also shows the wood grain at its best. Here, the honey-colored graining of the maple cabinets seems to almost shimmer, adding immeasurably to the look of the room. Every different wood has its own grain pattern, and you might even choose your cabinets based on the grain of the wood.

HARMONIZE BUILT-INS WITH CABINETS. If you're going to go with high-end cabinets such as those pictured here, you can enhance the kitchen design even more with custom built-ins fabricated to match. As is obvious in this room, a breakfast area with banquettes styled like the cabinets creates a seamless look that pleases the eye wherever it wanders. Many custom cabinet manufacturers provide fabrication services for other built-in elements—something worth keeping in mind if you're willing to consider the added expense of custom cabinets.

USE MID-RANGE WOOD TONES TO MODERATE DARKER SHADES. The black counters and stove, along with deep, olive-green wall paint, make this small kitchen a bit closed in. Blonde or light wood tones in the cabinets might have jarringly contrasted the darker elements of the design, but the mid-range cherry finish on these stylish cabinets effectively keeps things from being too visually heavy. Cabinet finishes are a great way to bend the kitchen design in one direction or another, because the cabinets usually cover quite a bit of visual surface area.

INTERMINGLE TO ADD POP. This small kitchen design was already a bit eclectic, with swirling metal tiles and island insets, modern fixtures, and a steel countertops, so mixing dark and blonde cabinets is all part of the fun. The contrast between the two—with the darker base cabinets keeping the design firmly rooted and the blond Euro-style cabinets complementing the nearly white wood floor—sets up visual tension that successfully walks the fine line between balance and discord.

ANNOUNCE TRADITIONAL STYLE WITH RICH FINISHES. The deep brown stain on these cabinets—in tandem with the traditional hardware—leaves no doubt as to the design theme of this traditional kitchen. Marble counters and the unusual addition of an undermount apron sink dress up the room, but the cabinets are the foundation of the design and of the style. If you're looking to create a recognizable style in your kitchen, look first at the correct cabinet finish for the period or theme.

SAY MODERN WITH "SLAB" DOORS. Flat-front doors go high style when you create them from maple and finish them blonde, as was done for this kitchen. Wraparound twin island granite countertops and matching wall cabinets give this modern space a very sleek aspect and wonderfully light and clean feel. The oversized frameless cabinets are not only incredibly beautiful, they also allow maximum access to the interior space, making them quite useful as well.

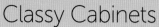

REPEAT INTERESTING FEATURES FOR MAX WOW. The scalloped bottom edge on these good-looking cottage kitchen cabinets are copied in both the top and bottom units. This is a great way to reinforce the design theme and to decorate what are otherwise fairly plain cabinets. The detail on the bottom of these units adds just enough flair in the curvy profile to spruce up the look without corrupting the design style.

INTRODUCE BEADBOARD TO BRING COUNTRY HOME. Beadboard works great as a wall covering, and just as well as side and back cabinet panels, as shown in this warm and welcoming country kitchen. The doors are mounted recessed into the face frames of the cabinets, which gives them a very trim appeal. But it's the beadboard recessed panels on the sides of the cabinets and the back of the peninsula island that reinforce the design theme. Cabinet sides and backs are often forgotten in the focus on cabinet door styles. That's a shame because, as this kitchen shows, they can represent a valuable design opportunity.

EMPHASIZE FINE POINTS FOR EXTRA FLAIR. These finely detailed cabinets have been finished with thin darker lines following the panel profile sections, which draws the eye to the incredible detail of the cabinet doors. The footed columns at each end of the cabinet run, and the matching dishwasher front, reinforce the reality that these are very high-end cabinets. A marble countertop is the perfect luxury addition to the sophisticated style of these units.

Classy Cabinets

PLAY WITH MOLDING TO CREATE A ONE-OF-A-KIND LOOK. Intricate molding details, such as the beading along the lower lip of the crown molding topping these traditional cabinets, can create a wholly unique look. It's a small detail with big visual impact. You'll find an amazing diversity of crown molding styles to top your cabinets. Choose a profile that holds its own without showing up the lines and form of the cabinets themselves.

MATCH COUNTERTOP TO CABINETS. Although you can choose a distinctive countertop material for your kitchen, it's easier to select cabinets and then match the countertop to the cabinets you've selected. Here, a perfect match is achieved between beige cabinets and a laminate countertop crafted to look like a travertine stone surface. The rough visual texture of the counter contrasts the smooth cabinet surface, but the colors are perfectly in sync—right down to the silver highlights in the counter that pick up on the silver cabinet pulls.

COLOR CABINETS GREEN FOR TIMELESS STYLE. Next to white, green is perhaps the favorite color for kitchen cabinets, and for good reason. The color carries with it associations of nature and can have a calming effect on a room that is often extremely busy in large household. A mid-range green such as this one—neither so bright that it strays into neon territory nor so somber that it dims the design—is ideal for a hue that will look good over time. This style of green with its modest black undertone is likely to look as good in five years as it does today.

INSTITUTE STATELY WITH GRAY. For as long as people have been decorating houses, grey has been used for its connotations of authority, dignity, and solemnity. If you're creating a sophisticated, high-end kitchen style such as the one shown here, grey is a natural tone for the cabinetry. Use a darker grey to hide dirt, wear, and tear. Regardless of the grey you choose, though, don't forget the details like the simple and elegant handles and pulls on these cabinets. You can also use glass fronts to provide some sparkle to an otherwise staid look.

Classy Cabinets

CREATE A CLEAN AIRY FEEL WITH BRIGHT WHITE. A pure white, like the shade used on these cabinets, makes for an upbeat feel in the kitchen. It also pretty much shouts cleanliness. A bank of glass cabinet doors is the perfect partner for white cabinets, because the interiors are usually white, and the glass adds sparkle to the bright surface of the cabinets. Small details, like the artfully designed dual faucets, provide even more visual interest. It's a sharp look that works well across kitchen design styles.

ACCENT FRAMELESS CABINETS WITH GLASS. A sleek contemporary kitchen like this one is all about subtle style. Solid colors, reflective surfaces, and simple straight lines all create an impressive look, but also one that can tend toward the sedate. Add a little spark to the design with a couple accent cabinet fronts, and you create the opportunity to show off vases, attractive dinnerware, and other visually interesting items. Use what's in the cabinet to display a few curves or a splash of color to contrast the rest of the design.

REFLECT A SMALL REALITY, SO THAT IT APPEARS LARGER. Using mirrors to make a small room seem much larger is an effective design strategy that's been used almost as long as people have been decorating homes. It can be just as effective in the kitchen as it is in other rooms, especially if you replace cabinet glass inserts with mirrored panels. The effect is glamorous, introducing extra brilliance and visually expanding the room—essential in a tiny kitchen like this.

SIZE GLASS FRONTS TO SUIT THE CABINETS. The skinny wall-mounted cabinets in this contemporary kitchen weren't large enough for full-size glass inserts, so the homeowner opted for decorative glass center columns. The glass has been etched with a double row design, which adds a bit of flair to the look. Single-panel inserts like this can be fairly easy to install, and can make a bigger impression than their modest sizes might indicate.

RETAIN TRADITIONAL STYLE WITH ISOLATED GLASS FRONTS. Glass fronts in all the upper cabinets in this kitchen would have interrupted the semi-formal look and drawn attention away from the rest of the design details. Instead, by using glass for only the top-most cabinet sections, the designer created display spaces that accent rather than overwhelm the design. This treatment is common in more formal kitchens, and custom cabinet manufacturers, such as the company that made these units, offer divided cabinets with glassed-in sections like these as part of their lineup.

OPEN UP A CRAMPED KITCHEN WITH GLASS ON BOTH SIDES OF A CABINET. This small cottage kitchen needs to maintain as much flow as possible to keep the space from becoming visibly closed in and claustrophobic. Using glass on both sides of the pass-through upper cabinets allows for light to transmit deep into the kitchen and provides a lovely visual of stacked dinnerware and attractive glassware. This also prevents the back of the cabinets from facing out or facing into the kitchen, something that would detract from any kitchen design.

MAKE YOUR KITCHEN ACCESSIBLE. Accessibility design involves creating kitchens with features that conform to the Americans with Disabilities Act and the best standards and practices of Universal Design. The idea is to make the whole space accessible to the disabled, elderly, and infirm who have trouble reaching high spaces, opening stiff doors, and performing other tasks the rest of us take for granted. The manufacturer of these cabinets, Freedom Lift Systems, crafts them to mount on motorized columns so that the shelves inside can be raised and lowered at the push of a button. They also produce countertops that can be raised and lowered, and base cabinet units with shelves that telescope out on mechanical arms. As with most accessible design cabinetry and countertops, these are offered in a selection of different finishes and styles.

Specialty Cabinet Storage

ADAPT SPECIALIZED STORAGE TO YOUR NEEDS. Got a dog and want to avoid the mess of dog food bags spilling all over? Use a pull-out cabinet insert such as the one shown here to collect large amounts of dog food and a few doggie treats. This double-pail feature could be used for recyclables or garbage just as easily as it serves as pet food storage. That's why cabinet features like this are incredibly useful and adaptable in any kitchen.

EXPLOIT SKINNY SPACES. Pull-out shelving custom sized for items such as spice jars, tins, or bottles are incredibly handy and make keeping your kitchen organized a breeze. These features are usually mounted with top and bottom slides that make the drawer easy to move out and in with a touch. The best thing is that they make great use of areas that would have otherwise been dead space. You'll even find full-height versions that can essentially serve as tall, skinny pantries!

PERFECTLY PLACE PULL-OUT SPICE ORGANIZERS. A custom spice rack like this is one of the nicest specialty storage features you can order from a custom cabinet manufacturer. Just be sure, though, that you can locate the spice rack close to a prep or cooking area. The convenience of the metal-slide-mounted feature will be somewhat negated if you have to walk across the room to get to the spices. Storage feature location should always be carefully thought out, to ensure these features are as convenient as possible.

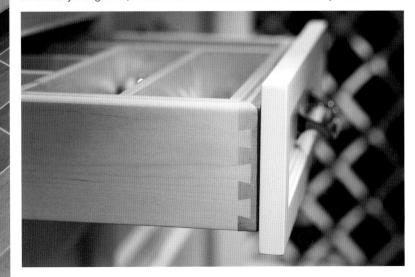

CHECK FOR QUALITY. Dovetailed joints are a sign of durable, well-made pull-out features—from drawers to spice racks and beyond. Solid wood boxes, hidden fasteners, and heavy construction are all signs of long-lasting, well-built cabinets and specialty features. A drawer like this will see a lot of use and it should open and close as easily years from now as it does on the day it was installed.

ADD A PULLOUT CUTTING BOARD. It doesn't matter if you're an avid foodie or just a weeknight hurry-up cook, cutting boards are essential additions to the kitchen. A pull-out hardwood cutting board like this one will add little expense to your custom cabinets, but will provide tons of convenience and ease when it comes to preparing meals. You can choose to add a cutting board right over a drawer, as shown here, or opt to place it over a tall base cabinet. Either way, use hardwood for the longest-lasting surface.

Specialty Cabinet Storage

EQUIP YOUR KITCHEN FOR ALL USERS. Universal Design is a term that describes home design features fabricated to make the home easier for those with disabilities and mobility issues to use. This cutting board is a prime example of a Universal Design feature. It can be extended far enough for a wheelchair to roll under, while still being steady enough to allow for chopping of vegetables. Kitchen cooks can prep food sitting down, or the board can just be used as any pullout cutting board would be. In any case, the greater surface area makes it even handier than other cutting boards.

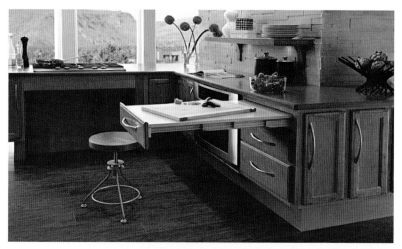

DESIGN TO ORGANIZE. When choosing kitchen cabinets and drawers, look for custom features that will make your life easier and keep your kitchen in order. Simple drawer organizers like these can be an amazing convenience and will help you ensure that everything in your kitchen has a place close to where the utensil, textile, or dishware will be used.

MAKE ACCESS EASY WITH EXPOSED DRAWERS. The large, deep pullout drawers in this kitchen island are just the thing to keep a wealth of pots and pans at the ready, right where they'll be used. Using drawers rather than a cabinet for this storage is a wise decision. The drawers circumvent the need to reach and they help keep the pots and pans organized. The same manufacturer that produced the cabinets in the rest of the kitchen—including the units in this island—produced the pull-out drawers. Most large cabinet manufacturers provide one-stop shopping by offering a full complement of storage options.

WEAVE YOUR WINE INTO YOUR CABINETRY. Wine bottles should be stored laying on their sides and kept secure from anywhere the bottles might be knocked over and broken. Storing wine above a cabinet is ideal, and is also a lovely decorative feature that makes any kitchen look sophisticated. The wine here is stored in a manufactured cabinet unit with room for glassware in glass-fronted cabinets below. The unit was installed in a kitchen alcove that is used as a mini bar area. This is an example of focusing the design of one area in the kitchen on one aspect of cooking and dining—a strategy that can work throughout the kitchen.

Specialty Cabinet Storage

SELECT CABINET FEATURES THAT SUIT YOUR LIFE. Do you keep cleaning products and lots of other materials under the sink? Then you might benefit from this specialized undersink cabinet. It has a specially formulated polymer base that won't be damaged by spills. A ridged surface ensures that everything stored under the sink is kept slightly above any moisture that might collect, and the entire cabinet box interior is extremely cleanable. Proprietary innovations like this can make your kitchen much more efficient, depending on how and where you want to store everything in the room.

USE DIVIDERS IN LARGE DRAWERS AS WELL AS SMALL. Although drawer dividers are most common for flatware and similar small-drawer items, adding dividers to larger drawers is also a great way to keep things in order. Incorporate pockets of different sizes and shapes to create the most usable space possible. Many dividers are also adjustable, giving you even more control over what you store where.

Handsome Racks & Shelves

DISPLAY COLOR WITH DISH RACKS. Built-in dish racks are an increasingly popular feature of custom cabinetry. It's a quaint element that can be useful for storing decorative dinnerware and platters. You'll get the most design oomph If you leave your white dishes inside a cabinet and use the dish rack to display more colorful plates and saucers, as the homeowner has done here.

ACCOMMODATE CULINARY PASSIONS. Simple stacked wine cubes are a great way to store a vast number of bottles and indulge your inner oenophile. These boxes are relatively easy to build, or they can be purchased through many different cabinet manufacturers. They can also fit in many different areas and configurations. If you want to make the look even more special, add interior cabinet lighting as was done here. The LED lights illuminate the bottles making them glow in jewel tones—all while making it easier to locate exactly the bottle you're craving.

DIVIDE ROOMS WITH OPEN SHELVING. Open shelving allows for the free flow of air and light, and gives a kitchen a more informal look. The open shelves in this room are used for display pieces, but could just as easily hold cookbooks, or cookware—anything that looks attractive from both sides. Even though you can see through shelves like this, they create a vivid visual border that helps define different areas in an open floor plan, such as the kitchen and dining area in this house.

IF YOU HAVE IT, FLAUNT IT! Alcove shelving is a wonderful alternative to installing cabinets. Alcoves lend themselves to shelves because shelves show the architecture to better advantage than a set of cabinets would. Cabinets would also be more difficult to install in the limited space of an alcove like this one. If you choose significant shelving area, like the space shown here, use it for the best-looking dinnerware, serving pieces, or glassware you own. The alcove becomes a kind of visual frame, drawing attention to whatever you put on the shelves. In this kitchen, the crisp white shelves work perfectly with the tiled backsplash and the dark tiles crafted to look like wood flooring.

COMBINE SHELVES AND CABINETS FOR CONTEMPORARY BLISS. The unique storage unit lining one wall of this super-cool space has a sliding front. Shelves on either side are used to display attractive bowls and vessels, while the center section is concealed behind the door. The homeowner has the option of changing the look and sliding the door over either end to expose the middle section. It's a very contemporary feature and also a design highlight.

Handsome Racks & Shelves

CHOOSE A TRADITIONAL POT RACK FOR EASIER COOKING. A basic, sturdy, over-island pot rack like the one shown here is not only an interesting addition to any kitchen design, it also makes pots and pans more accessible. Put the rack over a prep area or cooktop, and it's easy to grab the pot you need in a flash. This also frees up cabinet space that would have been poorly optimized to store awkwardly shaped cookware.

MIX SHELVES FOR A FUNKY AND FRESH LOOK. Wood shelves intermingle with stainless steel platforms in this upbeat kitchen with lime green walls. It's a lively look that brings fun to the design, and keeps utensils, plates, and more right at hand. Blonde wood goes especially well with stainless steel, creating a Euro-look that remains novel and airy long after it is installed.

USE AN UNUSUAL POT RACK AS VISUAL. Hanging pot racks come in all kinds of metals (and some woods), including high-gloss chrome, brushed nickel, and the incredibly distinctive copper shown here. It's a wonderful addition to a kitchen—especially if you're hanging copper pots or pans. The look works best with lighter wood cabinets or those that are finished in a stain that has red tones in it.

Handsome Racks
& Shelves

SLIDE INTO EURO-STYLE. Hanging bars are a great way to get utensils and other small kitchen essentials out in the open right where you use them. But the bars are also associated with the open, airy look of European or Scandinavian design. Use them when you are going for this look, especially when you've chosen freestanding cabinetry like the units shown in this dramatic kitchen.

ACCENT AN INDUSTRIAL LOOK WITH SLIDING BARS. Hanging bars can fit right into several different kitchen design themes, but they are naturally suited to pairing with raw materials, such as plank wood floors, a black recycled paper countertop, and the exposed brick walls like the mounting surfaces in this kitchen. The metal looks great against the imperfections and lines in the bare mortared structure, and the exposed kitchen tools reinforce the notion of this kitchen as a space where serious cooking takes place.

MAKE USE OF DEAD WALL SPACE. Hanging storage bars come in a range of lengths, so that you can use the length that best suits your available space. But when you have an open wall that begs for some ornamentation, fill it with the happy clutter of utensils and cookware by using the longest bars you can find. Be sure to position the bars for easy access—eye level for heavier or larger objects, and lower down for lighter utensils and cookware.

EXPLOIT BACKSPLASH WALL SPACE. You'll find completely integrated, all-in-one, wall-mounted hanging systems available from many different kitchen supply and general home retail stores. These are ideal for dressing up a large backsplash area, such as the stunningly glass-tiled surface in this kitchen. The systems include configurations with shelves, hanging bars, matching S hooks, and simple-to-install brackets. The look is neat and trim, and rather sleek as well. As this kitchen illustrates, it's a beautiful way to get a cooking area in order.

Breathtaking Appliances

Once upon a time, nobody thought of large kitchen appliances as decorative elements. In postwar kitchens across America, stoves, refrigerators, and dishwashers were all just workhorses meant for function—not for form. The aesthetic decision in buying a new stove or refrigerator basically hinged on choosing between white and off-white. Or, in the case of the forgettable, regrettable 1970s, avocado green. Fortunately, we've come a long way.

Today's appliances are anything but dull workhorses. Sleek stainless steel units have redefined the kitchen, making this room look more high-tech and sophisticated than ever before. Professional-quality gas stoves give foodies everywhere the chance to indulge their inner chefs, while making the kitchen look increasingly like a stylish restaurant workspace. New innovations continue to redefine the look of kitchen appliances, from cabinet-front panels that disguise a dishwasher or trash compactor, blending them into a row of cabinets, to window-front refrigerators that give us a peek inside before we ever open the door.

The point in all this is that today's appliances are every bit as much design elements as they are key players in food prep, cooking, and clean up. They are no longer just accommodated in the room; kitchens must now be designed with the look of the appliances in mind.

This means not only considering the appearance of essential appliances such as the stove or refrigerator, it also entails considering new luxury units that can add a whole new functional aspect to your kitchen. For instance, choose a wine refrigerator to nurture an interest in the wonders of the grape, or select a trash compactor to keep a busy kitchen as neat as a pin. The choices are wonderfully varied, so get shopping and be open to transforming both the look and function of your kitchen.

MAKE APPLIANCE SELECTION EASY WITH A SUITE. If you're after a coordinated look and don't want to mix and match, you can buy "suites" of appliances. Manufacturers produce appliance families comprising individual appliances designed to visually work together. As this kitchen illustrates, the matched look draws the viewer's eye through the room's design and creates a fluid, pleasing appearance. Not only do these appliances have the same stainless steel finish, the oblong windows and lines of the appliances are all coordinated as well.

COCOON YOUR REFRIGERATOR. Containing a refrigerator in a cavity is a common practice that hides the featureless sides of the unit and focuses attention on the well-designed face. This technique is especially effective when you're working with high-end, pro-quality units like the side-by-side freezer and refrigerator here, complemented by a wine refrigerator with door window. An alcove or setback of any sort becomes a frame to showcase gorgeous appliances like this.

Striking Refrigerators

BE SURE THE INSIDE OF A FRIDGE WORKS AS WELL AS THE OUTSIDE. You can find many different refrigerators with decorative panels to match cabinetry, as with the wood fronts on this unit. But while the look of your refrigerator has a big impact on the room's design, you also want to make sure that the refrigerator you buy accommodates what you need to store. This over-and-under model features a bottom drawer set up to accommodate common sizes of beverages and other specific food containers.

PUT THE REFRIGERATOR CENTER STAGE. Although it's common to minimize the appearance of a refrigerator, you can just as easily make it a stand-out focal point. This country kitchen design is rather demure, with its dark colors and simple lines. The stainless steel face of a high-tech three-door refrigerator brings a splash of brightness and style to the room without totally breaking up the country style. It's the star of the show, but not the only actor on stage.

BLEND YOUR REFRIGERATOR INTO THE ROOM. Appliance manufacturers now offer, as part of their upscale lines, the ability to match refrigerator fronts to existing cabinetry. This allows you to create a nearly seamless design that exploits beautiful surfaces like the heavily grained wood fronts in this kitchen. This particular model of refrigerator includes a window, adding to the allure and giving you a peek inside the refrigerator without having to open the door (which saves precious energy and lowers your monthly bill).

CUSTOMIZE FOR A CHIC UNIQUE LOOK. If you've set a high bar for your kitchen design, you might want to consider a totally custom installation like the one shown here. These mirror side-by-side units are a freezer on one side with a refrigerator on the other. Both are clad in the same wood paneling that covers the wall, with custom-made vent openings and handles in the same wood. This kind of detailing on an appliance is admittedly pricey, but it's also incredibly stunning and can be a jaw-dropping feature in any kitchen.

Dynamic Dishwashers & Compactors

HIDE A DISHWASHER. As with refrigerators, dishwasher manufacturers offer customized front panels to match the look of kitchen cabinets. This can help you create a seamless appearance along a row of base cabinets, especially those with handsome or uniquely finished doors. Less expensive dishwashers often come with multiple front panels that can be swapped out. Although these won't match your existing cabinetry exactly, they do allow you to change the look and find one that best suits your kitchen design.

FOR A CLEAN, FRESH LOOK. Sometimes, the appliance's façade works just fine in the design. In a bank of bright white cabinets, a stainless steel dishwasher looks right at home. The surface is not only bright and reflective, it is also easy to keep clean. And keep in mind that stainless steel appliance fronts are quickly becoming a classic and traditional look. Look for brushed or textured stainless steel if you have a lot of children in your house and you want to spend less time cleaning fingerprints off your appliances.

HIDE CONTROLS WHEN POSSIBLE. A grid of controls on the front of a dishwasher usually detracts from the look of the unit and makes it impossible to dress up the façade with any kind of special or custom panel. The better options are top-mounted controls, along the lip or edge of the unit. Many of today's more upscale appliances feature these kind of hidden controls, which leads to a much cleaner look in the kitchen. If you're going upscale with your design, it's a good idea to consider hidden controls.

POSITION A COMPACTOR WHERE IT LOOKS BEST. A trash compactor doesn't necessarily need to be in any one place in the kitchen (as opposed to a dishwasher that is normally placed right next to the sink). That's why you should look for a place to put it that makes the most visual sense. Positioned on the inside wall of a large island, a trash compactor is still conveniently at hand, but largely invisible to anyone but the cook. The homeowner here has placed the compactor in a run of standard-sized cabinets—the same size as the trash compactor. This creates a uniform visual rhythm that is pleasing to the eye, even though the compactor presents a different finish.

BLEND AN INDUCTION RANGE INTO THE COUNTER. This stainless steel induction cooktop reads as a blank reflective surface, matching the surface of the stainless steel countertops on either side. The combination creates a high-tech look that intimates serious cooking. This type of treatment takes some planning because the cooktop is nearly on level with the countertops. The surrounding darker surfaces emphasize the illusion.

TREND BLACK WHEN THE KITCHEN CALLS FOR IT. Black finishes are less common than stainless steel or white, but they do have a place in the right setting. Where you're after dark and dramatic, as in this kitchen, a black stove and microwave combination can top off the drama and make things sizzle in more ways than one. The luxury, frameless, cherry finish cabinets in this kitchen add a warm luster in contrast to the sleek high gloss surface of the appliances, setting up a modest dynamic tension and upping the visual interest in the room.

ADD MEGA CONVENIENCE WITH A BUILT-IN WARMING DRAWER. Cooktops are the height of luxury for an avid cook, but if you want to make the cooktop even more useful, install a warming drawer like this one, right below the cooktop. It's almost as easy as installing a cabinet drawer, although it does require wiring into the cooktop circuit. But with a little effort, you can keep food warm while you finish preparing that perfect meal for your next dinner party. Put the drawer behind a front that matches the surrounding cabinets to finish the feature in high style.

GROUP RANGES AND MICROWAVES. The reality is that microwaves are often used in conjunction with a range—say, to melt a key ingredient before it is added to a pot or pan. So it only makes sense to position them in close proximity. The accepted practice, where possible, is to mount the microwave right over the range. This entails a fan that sucks fumes from the cooktop back behind the microwave, but that's easy enough to have installed. When combining appliances in an arrangement like this, it works best if each has the same finish.

MAKE A HIGH-END RANGE A DESIGN CENTERPIECE. If you are spending the money and making the commitment to a restaurant-quality appliance like this, it only makes sense to shine the design spotlight on the unit. Here, the homeowner has positioned the range in front of an easy-to-clean and simply spectacular wall clad in stainless steel. A crowded pot rack overhead adds to the impression of a professional's kitchen, and the entire look is impressive and arresting.

WALL MOUNT FOR A TRIM LOOK AND SUPER CONVENIENCE. This wall-mount installation includes, from top to bottom, a microwave, stove, and warming drawer. The look is chic, with all the appliances contained in a single column topped by a handy cabinet. Notice the thick, sturdy handles that guarantee a sure grip on the doors, and high-tech controls that give the look some serious foodie cred. Stacking appliances like this is a great way to conserve space and create a cooking and baking center point in the kitchen.

CLUSTER KEY APPLIANCES FOR MAXIMUM EFFICIENCY. This is especially important in a small kitchen such as this. The placement of the range, refrigerator, and sink/dishwasher creates a tight work triangle that saves steps, time, and frustration and makes best use of three high-end appliances. Work lighting over each of the appliances makes them easier to use and highlights the stainless steel finish.

Fascinating Ovens, Cooktops & Ranges

INJECT STYLE WITH A HEAVY DUTY ELECTRIC RANGE. Electric ranges used to be the ugly sister in the kitchen, an also-ran to the restaurant styling of gas units. Not anymore. This high-end electric range includes the easy-to-grasp control knobs, sturdy feet, and rock solid construction you'd expect in a top-shelf gas unit. The looks are only one part of the equation; newer electric ranges are super quick to heat up and more exacting than ever in temperature ranges. If your current unit leads to spoiled meals, it may be time to upgrade your style and your cooking capacity.

ADD A HANDSOME DOUBLE-DUTY WORKHORSE. The classic, sturdy gas range look captured in the styling of this stunning unit is just part of the appliance's appeal. It's actually an efficient electric convection oven topped by a gourmet gas cooktop. These days, manufacturers not only offer an amazing array of looks for their appliances, they also provide all the functionality you could ask for.

PULL OUT THE STOPS WHEN COOKING IS YOUR LIFE. For a busy kitchen, or if you are just a chef-quality home cook, consider going big with a fully featured luxury gas range like the one shown here. Including a grill, six burners, and a double oven, this is serious cooking power for the serious cook. But it's also true eye candy, with an unusual matte black finish that matches both the hood and the other appliances in the kitchen. The finish plays perfectly against the yellow in the blonde cabinet finishes. You couldn't ask for a more stunning look in the kitchen.

MARRY GAS BURNERS AND STONE SURFACES. The appeal of iron grates set against a natural stone background is simply undeniable. Here, the intricate stone mosaic tile backsplash makes the sleek stainless steel pop, and the marble surfaces give the cooktop the perfect stage. This particular unit sports chunky red controls that are easy to use and provide a fun splash of color for the eye. As part of a suite of luxury stainless steel appliances, it completes a jaw-dropping kitchen design full of appealing natural materials that present a mix of textural effects.

Wonderful
Wine Refrigerators

TURN YOUR ISLAND INTO A BEVERAGE CENTER. The bookended refrigerators on this island provide a lot of refreshment as well as interesting visuals. The front doors match the oversized drawer fronts, and a wine refrigerator keeps vintage whites at the ready for any party (or just a stylish weeknight dinner). Slide-out drawers provide easy access to the bottles, and hidden controls give you the ability to adjust the temperature as desired. Luxury porcelain floor tile with a surprisingly convincing wood look completes a very pretty picture.

MAKE A SECONDARY SINK AREA SPECIAL WITH A WINE REFRIGERATOR. This small alcove is tiled in stunning style with glass mosaics that make the space sparkle. It calls for special appliances that can create something more than a bar sink area. A blue-lit wine refrigerator adds a bit of color and lot of convenience to the drinks zone. The stainless steel styling complements the crisp tile and exposed storage, and although it's modest in size, the refrigerator holds a good number of bottles—as many as any party might call for.

INDULGE YOUR PASSION WITH A FULL-SIZE WINE REFRIGERATOR. This unit features a top vent and interior-mounted temperature controls that leave the front glass door plain and elegant, with a wood frame that matches the surrounding cabinetry. Interior lights make it easy to find the bottle you're looking for without opening the door, and slide out trays provide effort-free accessibility to your wine collection. It's the height of luxury and convenience in wine storage and a tremendously sophisticated look.

Eye-Catching
Vent Hoods

GET CURVY FOR SEDUCTIVE APPEAL. Curved range hoods are less common than straight-line models, which makes them an unusual look in a contemporary kitchen. But they also bring a bit of drama and flair to kitchen designs featuring an abundance of straight lines and flat surfaces, such as this sleek space. Add glass ledges like those on this hood, and the hood becomes a truly distinctive design element.

ADD HANGERS FOR USABILITY AND PANACHE. The utensil hangers included on this hood are just one of several accessories that can be added to this cooktop hood. Buy one with directional lighting to illuminate different parts of the cooking area, or choose a hood with integral shelves to add attractive storage right near where you do your cooking.

INJECT WHIMSY WITH A CLAD HOOD. This country kitchen features stunning cabinetry that's true to style and understated, just as the countertops and walls are. But the nearly bell-shaped range hood is not only oddly proportioned, it's coated in a bright white enamel with metal strips outlining the shape. It's an interesting decorative element that if styled more traditionally, would have melted into the background. As it is, it brings a smile to the face of any visitor.

EXPLOIT HOOD AS ART.
Appliance manufacturers
keep an eye on design and
have made great strides
on the high end, turning
functional features into
design standouts. This
sleek, stunning perimetric
range hood is one example
of what's on offer if you're
willing to move to a higher
price range. The hood may
look like a designer plasma
TV, but it actually moves
significant air volume with
four speeds determined
by hidden controls.
The look is futuristic,
sleek, and undeniably
sexy, and few kitchens
wouldn't be improved
with the addition of this
jaw-dropping feature.

CONCEAL A HOOD FOR OVERHEAD STYLE. Nothing says you have
to use a range hood just as it appears. This hood is concealed behind
a simple façade decorated with an ornate tiled design. If your kitchen
style doesn't lend itself well to stainless steel surfaces or angular hood
construction—or if you just want to dress up the hood a bit—this is
a great alternative to a plain hood appearance. You can hide a hood
behind wood to match cabinetry, disguise it with glass tiles, or just
conceal it behind a painted drywall surface.

USE DUCTWORK FOR DRAMA. Kitchen hoods often vent directly
through a wall or through a drywall or cabinet column, meaning that
the ductwork is hidden. But in a modern or sleek contemporary design
that is all angles and lines, the ductwork itself can become something
of an impressive design element. This minimal kitchen features
breathtaking vaulted ceilings and a sweeping wall of windows, both of
which are perfectly complemented by a dramatically flared hood cowl
topped by a visually substantial duct column.

CENTRALIZE DESIGN FOCUS AROUND A CEILING-MOUNTED HOOD. Hanging range hoods require a great deal of planning, but usually give you the chance to customize the kitchen's layout. Here, the layout is logically arranged, with the prep, storage, and clean-up on one side, the cooking area anchored by a handsome overhead hood in the middle, and the eating and relaxing section on the near side. It's a thoughtful layout, and the range hood is both an attractive addition and one that helps clearly define the separation between kitchen areas.

SURPRISE THE EYE WITH SHINY. This eclectic kitchen was the perfect place to change up the look of the oversized hood, and what better way than to use a totally unconventional finish? The glossy surface of the polished metal hood adds some brightness to an otherwise dark room design, balancing the gorgeous dark wood island and cabinets. It also accentuates the shape and form of the hood, helping it visually pop off the wall. Changing the conventional can often bring a surprising freshness to kitchen designs.

SAY IT PROUD. Sometimes, it's best to use the appropriate range hood without adornment, special treatments, or concealment. This is a handsome, sturdy, high-quality hood that looks great against a tiled wall. The natural wood textures, stone, and glass all around it complement the look of the stainless steel, and the hood's simple, crisp lines do justice to the busy patterns in the space. It was a wise choice not to try to dress up this already upscale appliance.

TRY THE CHIMNEY EFFECT. A column hood can be an incredibly interesting feature in a modern kitchen. The modern lamp, porcelain floor tiles in a wood grain design, and solid-surface counter all boast simple forms. That's why a column-shaped hood fits right in. The hood motor and fan has been concealed in this fabricated shaft that was painted the same light grey as the walls.

Beautiful Fixtures

They might seem like small pieces of a much bigger picture, but a faucet and sink can make an indelible impression on any kitchen design. Like a refrigerator or lighting fixture, every true kitchen must have at least one sink and faucet. But that doesn't mean you have to limit yourself; larger kitchens often do well with a standard sink and faucet, and a second, smaller prep sink on an island or a long prep countertop. Either way, both sink and faucet are your chance to embellish the look of the kitchen and make working in the room a lot easier. There's just no getting around the fact that no matter how good the duo look, the sink-faucet combo is the center of all kitchen clean up.

The faucet is naturally going to be the more high-profile member of that duo. Faucets are like jewelry for the kitchen, and manufacturers have responded to the ever-growing hunger for new looks by producing faucets in an astounding number of finishes. You can find models in chrome, brushed nickel, stainless steel, enameled and plastic colors, antiqued bronze and iron, and more. The faucet's finish is naturally related to the form, and the form is indicative of the overall design style, from retro to country to modern.

Sinks have also come a long way from the simple choice of yesteryear between enameled white and stainless steel. These days, you'll find sinks in black, white, and colors as well as the continually popular stainless steel. On the low end, you can buy an acrylic sink in a range of colors, but you'll need to baby it because the material is easy to scratch and will melt under high heat. Stainless steel is a durable choice with a look that fits into just about any kitchen style. Go with a thicker gauge to ensure longevity. Solid-surface sinks can be fabricated right into a solid-surface countertop and the color goes all the way through, so scratches aren't a problem. Enameled cast iron remains popular as well, because the sink will take a lot of abuse (although you do have to keep an eye out for chipping).

The finish is only one side of the sinks' coin. You'll also be choosing between one, two, or three bowls, as well as picking a mounting style. Sinks can be self-rimming (also known as

SPLURGE FOR BIG VISUAL EFFECT. This highly detailed antique reproduction faucet is an incredible look for an otherwise middle-of-the-road country kitchen design. But the faucet emphasizes the roots of the kitchen's style, and the gleaming chrome finish is simply stunning. Pairing it with a brushed stainless steel sink means that the sink provides a handsome background for the faucet. It also means that the sink will be around as long as the faucet is, without showing any wear and tear.

ADORN WITH GRACE. If you're willing to spend a bit more on your faucet, you can add visual poetry to a modern or contemporary kitchen with a sleek modern faucet. As this example shows, the latest faucets are the height of style and feature an exceptional interpretation of the classic gooseneck arch. A block lever looks almost seamless with the faucet body when turned off, and is part of a sophisticated appearance that can help define a clean modern aesthetic.

top mount), with a lip that rests on top of the counter. Or you can choose an undermount sink, which makes for easy cleanup but requires a countertop that can be fabricated with an exposed inside edge. Apron-front sinks are yet another version, with a front face that is completely exposed. These are impressive kitchen additions that contain abundant room in a single bowl for cleaning larger pots and pans.

No matter what style, shape, or color you're considering, you'll want to pick your faucet and sink at the same time. Once installed, they become lifelong visual and working partners. Choose carefully, and you'll make your kitchen more efficient, more pleasant to work in, and a space that sparkles during cleanup and at other times as well.

Fashion-Forward Faucets

INJECT CLASSIC STYLE WITH A GOOSENECK. The shape shown here is the time-honored gooseneck faucet that allows for easy cleaning for deeper pots, because the neck arches over the edge of the pot to spray hot water down inside. But the shape is also an elegant form well-suited to accent traditional, country, and period-style kitchen designs. A shiny chrome finish is the classic finish for a gooseneck and the finish of choice if you're adding the faucet to a highly recognizable kitchen theme, such as a cottage kitchen. White enameled handles are a wonderful touch on any chrome faucet, one that also has historical roots.

DRESS UP CONTEMPORARY WITH A GOOSENECK VARIATION. This sharp, modern take on the classic gooseneck is minimal, sleek, and a treat for the eye. The smartly curving neck terminates in a pull-down head for ease of cleaning, and the single-lever stylized handle provides ease of use. The best faucets always combine function and style in a package that is undeniably eye-catching and a pleasure to use when it comes time for clean up.

STICK WITH SIMPLE. If your kitchen design focuses on uncomplicated lines, plain solid finishes, and lack of patterns, accent it with a basic and beautiful faucet like this understated model. Featuring a proprietary "lustrous metal" finish, this unit has a swooping handle that's easy to grab and a pull-down sprayer head that looks almost seamless with the rest of the neck when not in use. Keep in mind when buying single-hole mount faucets like this that many are offered with optional deck plates, in case you want to install the faucet in a sink or counter with more than one existing hole.

FIND A FINISH THAT SUITS YOU. Faucet manufacturers provide more finishes than ever before, and you can choose from conventional chrome to the matte black shown here. This faucet won't show dirt or fingerprints, and it's a standout against the background of a beige quartz countertop and backsplash and brushed metal sink. Picking a faucet finish to contrast other surfaces around it has to be done carefully, but when it works, the look is a surefire hit.

USE EXISTING CUES TO GUIDE FAUCET CHOICE. The angular contemporary faucet shown here combines some of the crisp lines and curves of the scintillating backsplash tile, as well as the simple elegance of a solid-colored, solid-surface countertop and plain stainless steel sink. Note how the sink's brushed finish makes the chrome faucet pop just a little bit.

Fashion-Forward Faucets

ESTABLISH A PRO LOOK WITH YOUR FAUCET. Do you cook—and consequently clean up—a lot? A professional-quality faucet like this will serve heavy duty cleanup needs, and brings a "serious kitchen" aesthetic to the sink area. A stainless steel coil neck allows for a lot of flexibility in moving the head around to clean larger or oddly shaped pots and pans. The spray head is multi-function to produce different sprays depending on what you're trying to clean, and a bridge between the body and head helps keep the head steady for hands-free cleaning. It's a look that's all about function, yet presents an enticing form.

Fashion-Forward Faucets

FIND A HANDLE WITH FLAIR. One of the big advances among modern kitchen faucets has been in handle technology. Not only are there a multitude of handle options from which you can choose, they accommodate a wider range of users than ever before and are thoughtful designs that eliminate frustration. For instance, this handle is operated only by turning forward, so that the user never bumps into the backsplash. A simple, yet essential, design feature. The icing on the cake is that the handle has been artfully designed to bring a splash of eye candy to the faucet and sink.

FINESSE OLD STYLE INTO A NEW DESIGN. The detailing of this faucet, sprayer, and soap dispenser trio borders on the whimsical but hails from yesteryear. It's an antique look that can find new life in a contemporary or traditional kitchen, such as the room shown here. It's important that a faucet this distinctive carefully complement at least one other fixture or design element in the room—as this faucet does the drawer pulls on the cabinetry. A brushed finish makes the ornate fixtures just a little more subtle, but this is a dynamic look that can delight the eye in the right setting.

Fashion-Forward Faucets

CHOOSE A FORM THAT SUPPLIES. This low-profile, single-handle faucet sports an aerodynamic shape that is perfectly in keeping with the ridged-deck enameled sink and green glass backsplash. But more importantly, the pull-out head reaches somewhat further than a pull-down head on a gooseneck faucet, giving the homeowner more flexibility in spraying down dirty counters alongside the sink. There's always a balance to be struck in choosing a faucet, between the perfect look and a unit that serves exactly the way you want it to.

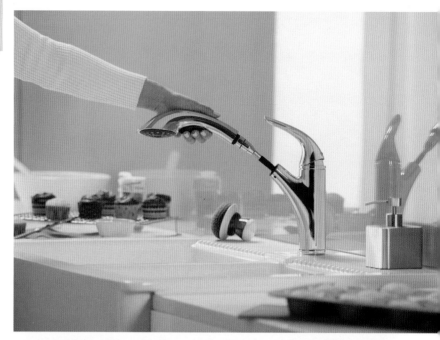

PICK POT FILLERS FOR FLAIR. A pot-filler faucet provides an extendable arm to bring water to the stovetop and fill deep pots for pasta or other dishes. These can be handy in busy or big family kitchens, but they should never be dull. The easiest way to add a pot filler into the kitchen design is to match the finish to surrounding design elements. The wall-mounted faucet here was intentionally chosen with a stainless steel finish that works with the backsplash, hood, shelves, and even the stunning glass tile on the wall. It's an amazingly coordinated look and the pot filler faucet fits right in.

CONSIDER PROFILE. Shopping for faucets usually means looking at them from the front. But if you're going to be equipping a sink in an island, it's wise to consider how the faucet looks from the side. This particular design presents a nearly seamless appearance in profile. The pull down head is perfectly in line with the curving neck and the handle seems to almost disappear into the lines of the body when viewed from the side. It's a small thing, but the small details of a kitchen design can make or break the look.

CHOOSE LOW-PROFILE FOR CONTEMPORARY. The more contemporary swan's curve of this faucet is a bit of an edgier look that is right at home with a sliding glass sink cover featuring an etched design and the high-tech brushed steel sink. This particular faucet is a center post mount, but includes a decorative deck plate that balances out the sweeping look of the neck and head. That feature would also make this a great choice for a pre-existing three-hole deck or sink, and the faucet is ideal for any modern or streamlined kitchen.

OUTFIT YOUR SINK FOR SUPER DUTY. This double-bowl stainless steel unit has a sturdy top ledge that will stand up to some rough treatment, but the real sell of the sink is the removable drain grates. This means you can pile in dishes, pans, and pots without every worrying about whether the sink will continue to drain. It's a nice extra feature that makes cooking cleanup just a little bit easier, and makes this sink just a little bit more special.

CHOOSE BOWLS BASED ON CLEANING. This stainless steel sink is a lovely look, with an appealing rounded shape and two different-sized bowls. The homeowner uses the larger of the two for cleaning large cookware like pots and pans or platters. The smaller sink is usually reserved for food prep and washing hands. It's also worth noting that the homeowner has opted for an undermount sink, a great choice with a solid-surface countertop like this recycled glass surface, which is the same color and texture all the way through. Because the sink is beneath the edge of the counter, food can be just wiped into the sink—no fuss, no muss.

MATCH FAUCET COLOR TO A SOLID-SURFACE SINK. This sink is fabricated right into the structure of the countertop, and the entire surface is a timeless soft white. Solid-surface sinks are colored all the way through, so scratches or other marks can be buffed out, and the sink is extremely durable in any case. But this look is especially effective based on the matching faucet. This sleek, single-handle unit has a white body that matches the sink and makes the whole look seamless, minimal, and modern.

OUTFIT YOUR SINK FOR SPECIAL STORAGE. You wouldn't think the bowl of a sink could provide storage, but you'd be wrong. With larger stainless steel sinks—especially those in an island or serving as a second sink—the sink may never be used to capacity for cleaning large cookware. Take the opportunity of the extra room to keep sponges, soaps, and other essentials like pot brushes off the countertop. Specialized in-sink containers are offered by several manufacturers to help you work efficiently and keep the sink area tidy.

Swanky Sinks

REINVENT THE CLASSIC APRON SINK. You should always keep your options open to borrowing and recasting signature features from other kitchen design styles. This clean and crisp contemporary kitchen is made even more beautiful with the addition of a stunning stainless steel apron-front sink. This twist on the tried-and-true farmhouse sink bends the form to contemporary surroundings, making the typical rounded shape crisp and linear. In addition to being a witty spin on a recognizable form, this sink also offers a tremendous amount of room inside to clean whatever might get dirty.

CREATE A MINI-THEME WITH YOUR SINK AND FAUCET. This kitchen is not overtly one design style or another, but the sink area is all about country farmhouse. With a patterned-apron farmhouse sink and an antiqued bronze finish on the double-handle gooseneck faucet and accessories, the look is very clear. It's also enough of a modest feature to fit right in with the rest of the kitchen, while adding a flash of style.

BUILD A DYNAMIC DUO. This stunning faucet features a coiled steel neck that allows the spray head to be directed where needed, with a lock bar that keeps it in place over the sink when flexibility is not needed. The solid-surface sink includes two bowls and a work surface, all in the same durable material that will stand up to a lot of abuse. The form of the sink accommodates a colander insert and a drain grid, both of which make food prep and cleanup easier. The combination of faucet and sink make preparing gourmet meals a cinch and create a stunning visual for the kitchen.

Incredible Islands

The ever-useful island has become the centerpiece of today's kitchen. Regardless of design style or kitchen size, an island can replace the need for a kitchen table, makes working in the kitchen easier, adds accessible storage to the room, and much, much more. Although they aren't appropriate for very small kitchens, every other kitchen can usually benefit from the addition of an island.

Islands can be built-in or freestanding, substantial or modest. Regardless, the place to start is with the size you need.

A kitchen island should be big enough to accommodate whatever you hope to do on the island, and small enough that it doesn't impede foot traffic in the kitchen. The commonly accepted rule of thumb is to leave at least 36 inches of space on all sides of an island, although 42 inches is a better baseline for a busy kitchen. The idea is to ensure the island doesn't block cabinet or appliance door swing, and that two people can comfortably pass anywhere next to the island.

Island shape goes hand in hand with size and has a big effect on how the island is visually perceived. A rectangle is the most common shape for kitchen islands because it suits so many different kitchen layouts. Square islands may serve better where space is limited, but the shape is more boring. Round islands, although rare, can be a stellar design feature in the right kitchen (but you lose valuable prep space with the loss of corners).

Ultimately, your island can be whatever your imagination makes it. Install a cooktop to create a convenient cooking area, fabricate a breakfast bar to accommodate diners or friends sharing a drink and a chat, or install a sink for extra cleanup capability. Whatever its function, tie your island to the rest of the kitchen with compatible countertop surfaces, base cabinet finishes, or overall style.

MAINTAIN PROPORTION. Here, a big, bright, white kitchen is well served with a stunning centerpiece island. The island is visually tied to the rest of the room through the use of matching granite countertops. The styling of the base perfectly matches the footed style of the cabinets throughout the kitchen. The size is right, too: the island leaves enough space for navigation but doesn't appear lost in the huge floor space of this kitchen.

DON'T FEAR FUNCTION-FREE ISLANDS. Sometimes all you need is a bit more prep surface and a smidge more storage. When that's the case, there's no need to overthink your island. Adding sinks or cooktops usually means new plumbing or electrical work, so an island like this one—with its modest size, simple countertop, and basic combination of one cabinet and open space—can serve perfectly in the kitchen. Styled like the other storage and surfaces in the room, an island like this can blend right into the design while still adding attractive form and furnishing to the kitchen.

USE A PENINSULA WHERE ISLANDS DON'T FIT. This long narrow kitchen wasn't a candidate for an island, but a peninsula extension off the end of the countertop serves the room perfectly. The peninsula is literally and visually tied to the rest of the design, provides extra seating and dining space, increases the storage capacity of the kitchen, and adds an interesting angle to the layout. Peninsulas can be wonderful additions to any kitchen where an island would be awkward.

CLEAN UP ON AN ISLAND. Because they are usually centrally located, islands are just about the perfect place for a sink—either the primary sink in the kitchen or a smaller ancillary sink for food prep and smaller messes. You do have to run plumbing for the sink, but once the water supply and drain are in place, you have the option of adding in a dishwasher like the one in this island. Take care in choosing a sink and faucet because they'll be on permanent display in the center of the kitchen. A stunning duo like those shown here are well worth the investment.

Island Magic

MAKE YOUR ISLAND DISTINCTIVE. You can choose to create a distinctive look with the island in your kitchen, as long as it meshes with the look of the other decorative elements. The impressive island in this kitchen features fine woodworking details and a signature pine grain, but the exceptional wood base marries well with the country-style high-end cabinetry and muted colors in the room. The countertop matches the other countertops in the room, as well as the seats on the stools, and helps tie the look together.

COMBINE WORK SURFACE AND SINK. This stunning modern faucet sets off an innovative stainless steel sink design. A durable safety glass panel slides along the top edge of the sink to open and close as needed. When closed, it can be used as a cutting board and neatly conceals the sink. Open, it allows for easy cleanup of food prep by wiping it right into the bowl of the sink. Simple dual-use solutions like this are great in smaller kitchens, where prep space will be at a premium.

ADD PORTABILITY TO INCREASE USEFULNESS. Although most islands are secured to the floor in one way or another, a sturdy wheeled island like this marble-topped wood unit can offer a lot of advantages in the right kitchen. The mobility allows you to put the work surface exactly where you want it at any given time. This can make food prep and cooking much easier. You can also move the island entirely out of the way when you want more room to move around. This style of island is usually less expensive than a built-in unit and, as this example shows, it can still supply plenty of usable storage.

Lighting the Kitchen Design

Light is the most important design element in a kitchen. If you doubt it, just try turning all the lights off some night and see how well the kitchen's design holds up in the dark! But lighting is much more than a simple design element in the kitchen; the proper lighting is crucial in making working, eating, and navigating in the kitchen easier and safer. You can even use lighting to create different moods at different times. Of course, that all depends on what type of light you're working with.

There are two basic types of light in any kitchen: The natural illumination from windows, skylights, and adjacent rooms, and the artificial light from the lighting fixtures. Artificial light can be further broken down into general, or "ambient," light sources, work or task lighting, and accent lighting that highlights specific design features. The best kitchen designs include a balance of all three of these in a design technique called "layering."

Getting that mix right can be made complex by the fact that different light bulbs provide distinctively different types of light. Light fixtures themselves can be largely hidden or become part of the design—sometimes, a big part.

Chances are, your natural light is pretty much determined by the windows you have. You may be able to install a skylight or solar tube, but for the most part, taking advantage of natural light means designing around the sunlight that comes in during the day.

Artificial light, on the other hand, is a design feature that requires just as much thought, consideration, and shopping as any other feature or fixture. In fact, because it's usually fairly easy to swap out light fixtures or locate new artificial lighting, you may find yourself regularly changing your fixtures as a way of updating the look of the kitchen. However, you always want to maintain proper layering of light in the space to maintain safety and comfort. Get your kitchen lighting right, and you'll not only be illuminating the room, you'll be making the design even more beautiful.

OPTIMIZE NATURAL LIGHT. Where appropriate and affordable, a long arched skylight like this can flood the kitchen with natural light all day. The skylight can also provide a view of the stars at night and, in conjunction with a wall of windows on the side of the kitchen, visually opens up the kitchen, making it seem much larger. Three overhead hanging fixtures light up the skylight well during the evening hours. Notice that the designer hasn't forgotten the need for layers of artificial light. They have supplemented the hanging "ambient" light fixtures with undercabinet task lighting, interior cabinet accent lighting, and ambient wall sconces.

SLICE THE SKY. A series of small skylights (these are non-operable) can pack as much punch as a much larger single unit. These three skylights scatter sunlight across the space during the course of the day and bring as much visual fireworks as a larger single unit would, quite possibly at a lower cost.

Alluring Windows & Skylights

ADD LEADED GLASS FOR A DISTINCTIVE LIGHT-TRANSMITTING DECORATION. Stained glass is a wonderful accent in the right kitchen, especially one that mixes design influences like the room pictured here. The color in stained glass won't fade or erode, and when used in a detailed window design, the stained glass comes to life when lit (and has an entirely different personality when not illuminated). Because the glass can mute light, it's wise to use a decorative stained glass window among other windows to maintain adequate levels of sunlight during the day.

DON'T BLOCK SINK WINDOWS. A window in back of the sink is a fairly common arrangement in today's homes and kitchens, because it provides a pleasing view from a busy workspace, as well as wealth of light to make sure everything is properly cleaned. It's also wise to use operable windows in this location, as another means for venting the kitchen during cooking or whenever smells or smoke threaten to overwhelm the room.

LIMIT LIGHT BLOCKING WHEN WINDOWS ARE FEW. This Euro-style galley kitchen receives moderate direct daylight courtesy of a single double-hung window. The homeowner uses a sheer window covering that will ensure privacy when necessary, but won't prevent light transmission even when the shade is down. Keep illumination in mind whenever you are choosing kitchen window treatments.

CONTROL NATURAL LIGHT. As lovely as natural light is, sometimes there can be too much of a good thing. A glass door and bank of counter-to-ceiling windows supplies plenty of sunlight during the course of the day, but can also heat up this south-facing kitchen. The answer is simple: Black-out cellular shades that can be raised and lowered with the pull of a cord. Always try to maintain as much control over the natural light in your kitchen as you have over the artificial light.

BRING THE SUNLIGHT TO THE KITCHEN. Even if your kitchen isn't directly below the roof, you can route the sunshine to the room with the help of a tubular skylight like the one shown here. These special fixtures use a reflective flexible tube that runs from the roof down as far as necessary to the ceiling of the kitchen. The result is a warm splash of light throughout the day—and you can even add a decorative effect by using one of the special lenses manufacturers offer, such as a prismatic lens.

LIGHT THE RIDGE. If you have cathedral ceilings or vaulted construction like this A-frame, a ridge skylight can be an unparalleled lighting and design feature. Although it doesn't appear to take up a lot of the ceiling area, because of the angles, it gathers an abundance of sunlight. And the look is simply incredible; it visually opens up the kitchen during the day and provides a starlit vista at night.

CONSIDER SURFACES IN CHOOSING FIXTURES. The gorgeous copper ceiling in this country kitchen is a highly reflective surface that amplifies any light source in the room. Understated, low-power ceiling fixtures and wall sconces provide all the ambient light the room will need, given the reflective power of the ceiling. Always keep surfaces in mind when choosing fixtures and light bulb wattages. The well-appointed cabinetry, cozy country colors, and antique stove all call for a warm incandescent light— halogen bulbs would have been a little too harsh for the surroundings.

TILE BACKSPLASHES FOR A BRIGHT WASH OF LIGHT. Glass tiles can be the perfect choice for backsplashes meant to reflect modest undercabinet lighting fixtures. The simple glass tiles on this backsplash really pop when the undercabinet lights come on, creating a spotlight feature that provides work surface illumination and a pretty visual to boot.

Smart Lighting Fixtures

COMBINE PENDANTS AND TRACK LIGHTS FOR AN ALL-IN-ONE SOLUTION. These stylish pendants are suspended over an island, but powered by an overhead track that also holds two adjustable track heads. The pendants can be positioned anywhere along the track, as can the two additional heads, providing a great deal of design flexibility. The track also creates a nice curvy graphic overhead, which adds to the impression the bell-shaped pendants make. And, in the end, it's much easier to wire in a single track than three pendants and a track.

PLAY IT SAFE BY MATCHING FIXTURES THROUGHOUT. Hanging fixtures or ceiling fixtures that will work in one part of the kitchen will usually go perfectly in other parts as well. As this example shows, you can visually tie different areas of the kitchen together by using the exact same overhead fixtures throughout the kitchen. This is also a way to take advantage of bulk discounts. Here's a tip though: If you're using pole mounted fixtures like those used in this kitchen, make sure the poles can be adjusted in length or cut, so that you can customize how far they hang down to suit the location and your desired look.

BLEND PUCKS INTO CABINETRY. LED "puck" lights are a great solution for undercabinet lighting and they keep work surfaces well illuminated. But some kitchen designs would be diminished with the pucks projecting below the cabinet bottom line. The answer is to buy puck lights in a color that matches the cabinets, so that they visually blend right into the cabinet and are relatively invisible when the lights are off.

LAYER KITCHEN LIGHTING. Design experts use the term "layering" to describe the ideal lighting scheme for this busiest of rooms. This means you need to first establish well-dispersed general (or "ambient") lighting, achieved with the ceiling fixtures in this kitchen. Task lighting comes next, illuminating key work areas around the room, as with the lighting pendants over the island cooktop and the undercabinet lights here. Last is the layer of accent lighting that decorates as well as illuminates. The toe-kick, under-counter LEDs, and cabinet lighting all fall into this last category. Combine all the layers and you get a warm, beautifully lit scene like this ideal kitchen.

ALLOW PUCK LIGHTS TO SHOW FOR A TRENDY FEEL. Puck LED lights are often concealed behind the lower ridge of cabinetry face frames, but that's not a hard and fast rule. In fact, exposed puck lights can look quite cool in the right setting. The white fixtures on the left perfectly complement the upscale glass backsplash tiles and blonde cabinetry. The metal pucks on the right give this modern black-and-white kitchen a little extra flare and really bring the shimmering black backsplash tiles to life.

Smart Lighting Fixtures

LIGHT STORAGE FOR DRAMA. Glass fronted cabinets and exposed shelves are great places to display beautiful glassware, bowls, serving pieces, and other specialty items in the kitchen. But darkened cabinets and shelves don't display notable pieces to their best advantage. That's why accent lighting in shelves and glass-front cabinets can exploit the spaces and bring a whole new aspect to the kitchen at large. The small accent lighting in this kitchen creates spotlights of interest that lead the eye through the room, but definitely gives extra attention to what's in the wall-mounted cabinets and shelves.

DECORATE WITH SPECIALTY LIGHTING. This visually busy kitchen has a lot of details worth highlighting, and the halogen recessed ceiling lights do a good job of showing off the shimmering wood floor grain and Asian-inspired Craftsman-style woodwork elements. But the fascination is really supplied by the purple lights illuminating an art panel behind the cooktop, and shining purple light showcasing a decorative plate on the counter opposite the stove. Use specialty or accent lighting in this way to really make a space your own.

PICK PENDANTS FOR FORM AS WELL AS LIGHT. The selection of pendant lamps on the market seems almost limitless, and you'll find them in every design style imaginable, and in different materials, from glass to paper to metal and beyond. Although they must first and foremost provide the amount and type of illumination you need wherever you intend to hang them, you can select a style that not only complements the rest of your kitchen design but—as with these three pendants—provides stunning focal points all on their own.

Accenting the Kitchen

Small accents are a way for you to make your kitchen design uniquely your own. These elements may be modest in size, but they can make a big impact on the overall design, and can take a design from simple to chic in a heartbeat. The really good news is that because they are usually inexpensive, accents won't break the bank if you opt for high-end materials and finishes.

The most obvious—and essential—accents are the hardware that goes on cabinets and drawers. Handles, pulls, hinges, and knobs are all design flashpoints that can draw attention to themselves or not. There are so many different variations for each of these that the hardest part is sifting through all the options facing you. Choose correctly and these tiny accents can even bring new life to old cabinetry.

But accents don't stop at the hardware on your cabinets. Wine racks, small appliances, and even clocks up the ante by incremental degrees, each addition putting a little more polish on your style.

If you're still working on the look of your kitchen or thinking about shifting up the style in one direction another, you can accent the look to make it just right. Just use portable features like glass racks, trays, spice racks, or bowls, which can be swapped out if you decide on a different design direction.

MAKE A BIG IMPACT WITH COLORED KNOBS. You can customize cabinet hardware to suit your needs as the homeowner here has done. This kitchen borders a children's play area in a large kitchen, and the wooden cabinet door knobs, painted in matte primary colors, inject a healthy dose of fun and visual interest. The bright white cabinets, warm vinyl floor (in a surprising diagonal wood plank appearance), and simple wood counters all keep the design honest and ensure that the burst of colors doesn't look jarring or clownish. It's an upbeat, sunny, and happy look full of natural charm.

SURPRISE THE EYE. What looks like a stylish secret cubby hole is actually a chic way to gather recipe trimmings for composting. A compost pile is a great way to feed your garden and help the environment, but collecting kitchen waste has usually been something to hide. Not anymore. This sleek unit pops right into a hole in the countertop, and is covered with a stainless steel lid. When the container gets full, just remove it and take it out to the compost pile. This is a great way to make a design plus out of something that would otherwise be a minus.

Photo Credits

Page 4: Photo courtesy of Formica Corporation, www.formica.com
Page 5 top: Photo courtesy of Kohler, www.us.kohler.com
Page 5 bottom left: Photo courtesy of GE Appliances, www.geappliances.com
Page 5 bottom right: Photo courtesy of GE Appliances, www.geappliances.com
Page 6: Photo courtesy of Merillat, www.merillat.com
Page 7 top left: Photo courtesy of Blanco America, www.blancoamerica.com
Page 7 bottom left: Photo courtesy of Top Knobs, www.topknobs.com
Page 7 right: Photo courtesy of tiella, www.tiella.com
Page 8 top: Photo courtesy of Sub-Zero, www.subzero-wolf.com
Page 8 bottom: Photo courtesy of Brooks Custom, www.brookscustom.com, 800-244-5432
Page 9 top: Photo courtesy of American Standard, www.americanstandard-us.com
Page 9 bottom: Photo courtesy of American Standard, www.americanstandard-us.com
Page 10: Photo courtesy of Cambria USA, www.cambriausa.com
Page 11: Eric Roth, photographer, www.ericrothphoto.com
Page 12 top left: Photo courtesy of Urban Homes, www.uhny.com
Page 12 top right: Photo courtesy of Formica Corporation, www.formica.com
Page 12 bottom: Photo courtesy of Canyon Creek Cabinet Company, www.canyoncreek.com
Page 13 top: Photo courtesy of KraftMaid, www.kraftmaid.com
Page 13 bottom: Photo courtesy of Brooks Custom, www.brookscustom.com, 800-244-5432
Page 14 top: Photo courtesy of Wilsonart International, www.wilsonart.com
Page 14 bottom: Photo courtesy of Plato Woodwork, Inc., www.platowoodwork.com
Page 15 top: Photo courtesy of Merillat, www.merillat.com
Page 15 bottom: Photo courtesy of Granite Transformations, www.granitetransformations.com
Page 16 top: Photo courtesy of Ikea Home Furnishings, www.ikea.com
Page 16 bottom: Photo courtesy of Jenn-Air, jennair.com
Page 17 top: Photo courtesy of LivedIn Images, www.livedinimages.com
Page 17 bottom: Photo courtesy of Interstyle Ceramic + Glass, www.interstyle.ca, 800-944-2904
Page 18 top: Photo courtesy of Juno Lighting Group, www.junolightinggroup.com
Page 18 bottom left: Photo courtesy of Danze, Inc., www.danze.com
Page 18 bottom right: Photo courtesy of GE Appliances, www.geappliances.com
Page 19: Photo courtesy of Enclume, www.enclume.com, 877-362-5863
Page 20 top: Photo courtesy of Cambria USA, www.cambriausa.com
Page 20 bottom: Photo courtesy of Canyon Creek Cabinet Company, www.canyoncreek.com
Page 21 top: Photo courtesy of GE Appliances, www.geappliances.com
Page 21 bottom: Photo courtesy of Formica Corporation, www.formica.com
Page 22 top: Photo courtesy of Plain & Fancy Custom Cabinetry, plainfancycabinetry.com
Page 22 bottom: Photo courtesy of Vetrazzo, www.vetrazzo.com
Page 23 top: Photo courtesy of Sub-Zero, Inc. and Wolf Appliance, Inc., www.subzero-wolf.com
Page 23 bottom: Photo courtesy of The Solid Wood Cabinet Company, www.solidwoodcabinets.com, 855-277-4820
Page 24: Photo courtesy of Ikea Home Furnishings, www.ikea.com
Page 25 top: Photolibrary, Karyn Millet, www.photolibrary.com
Page 25 bottom: Photo courtesy of Kichler Lighting, www.kichler.com, 866-558-5706
Page 26: Photo courtesy of DeWitt Designer Kitchens, www.dewittdesignerkitchens.com, (626) 792-8833
Page 27 left: Photo courtesy of Blanco America, www.blancoamerica.com
Page 27 right: Photo courtesy of GE Appliances, www.geappliances.com
Page 28 top: Photo courtesy of Globus Cork, www.corkfloor.com, 718-742-7264
Page 28 bottom left: Photo courtesy of Brooks Custom, www.brookscustom.com, 800-244-5432
Page 28 bottom right: Photo courtesy of Merillat, www.merillat.com
Page 29 top: Photo courtesy of Jenn-Air, jennair.com
Page 29 bottom: Photo courtesy of Plain & Fancy Custom Cabinetry, plainfancycabinetry.com
Page 30: Photo courtesy of KraftMaid, www.kraftmaid.com
Page 31 top: Photo courtesy of Interstyle Ceramic + Glass, www.interstyle.ca, 800-944-2904
Page 31 bottom: Photo courtesy of Richlite, www.richlite.com, 888-383-5533
Page 32 top: Photo courtesy of Cosentino USA, www.silestoneusa.com, 866-268-6837
Page 32 bottom: Photo courtesy of Kohler, www.us.kohler.com
Page 33 top: Photo courtesy of Kichler Lighting, www.kichler.com, 866-558-5706
Page 33 bottom: Photo courtesy of Kohler, www.us.kohler.com
Page 34 top: Photo courtesy of KraftMaid, www.kraftmaid.com
Page 34 bottom: Photo courtesy of GE Appliances, www.geappliances.com
Page 35 top: Photo courtesy of Elkay, www.elkay.com
Page 35 bottom left: Photo courtesy of GE Appliances, www.geappliances.com
Page 35 right: Photo courtesy of Enclume, www.enclume.com, 877-362-5863
Page 36 top: Photo courtesy of KraftMaid, www.kraftmaid.com
Page 36 bottom: Photo courtesy of KraftMaid, www.kraftmaid.com
Page 37 top: Photo courtesy of Viking, www.vikingrange.com
Page 37 bottom: Photo courtesy of Plain & Fancy Custom Cabinetry, plainfancycabinetry.com
Page 38: Photo courtesy of KraftMaid, www.kraftmaid.com
Page 39 top: Photo courtesy of Viking, www.vikingrange.com
Page 39 bottom: Photo courtesy of The Solid Wood Cabinet Company, www.solidwoodcabinets.com, 855-277-4820
Page 40 top: Photo courtesy of Poggenpohl, www.poggenpohl.com
Page 40 bottom: Photo courtesy of Formica Corporation, www.formica.com
Page 41 top left: Photo courtesy of Blanco America, www.blancoamerica.com
Page 41 bottom left: Photo courtesy of Bosch Home Appliances, www.bosch-home.com/us, 800-944-2904
Page 41 bottom left: Photo courtesy of Top Knobs, www.topknobs.com
Page 42 top: Photo courtesy of Vetrazzo, www.vetrazzo.com
Page 42 bottom: Photo courtesy of Cosentino USA, www.silestoneusa.com, 866-268-6837
Page 43 top: Photo courtesy of Jenn-Air, jennair.com

Page 43 bottom left: Photo courtesy of GE Appliances, www.geappliances.com
Page 43 bottom right: Photo courtesy of Pyrolave, www.pyrolave.fr
Page 44 top: Photo courtesy of Forbo Flooring Systems, www.forbo-flooring.com
Page 44 bottom: Photo courtesy of Interstyle Ceramic + Glass, www.interstyle.ca, 800-944-2904
Page 45: Photo courtesy of Formica Corporation, www.formica.com
Page 46 top: Eric Roth, photographer, www.ericrothphoto.com
Page 46 bottom: Photo courtesy of KraftMaid, www.kraftmaid.com
Page 47 top: Photo courtesy of Crown Point Cabinetry, www.crown-point.com, 800-999-4994
Page 47 bottom: Photo courtesy of American Standard, www.americanstandard-us.com
Page 48 top: Photo courtesy of Jenn-Air, jennair.com
Page 48 bottom: Photo courtesy of Top Knobs, www.topknobs.com
Page 49: Photo courtesy of Plain & Fancy Custom Cabinetry, plainfancycabinetry.com
Page 50: Photo courtesy of Walker Zanger, Inc., www.walkerzanger.com
Page 51 top: Photo courtesy of Crown Point Cabinetry, www.crown-point.com, 800-999-4994
Page 51 bottom left: Photo courtesy of Enclume, www.enclume.com, 877-362-5863
Page 51 bottom right: Photo courtesy of Viking, www.vikingrange.com
Page 52: Photo courtesy of DeWitt Designer Kitchens, www.dewittdesignerkitchens.com, (626) 792-8833
Page 53 top: Photo courtesy of Elkay, www.elkay.com
Page 53 bottom: Photo courtesy of Elkay, www.elkay.com
Page 54 top: Photo courtesy of Interstyle Ceramic + Glass, www.interstyle.ca, 800-944-2904
Page 54 bottom left and right: Photo courtesy of Kohler, www.us.kohler.com
Page 55: Photo courtesy of Vetrazzo, www.vetrazzo.com
Page 56 top left: Photo courtesy of Viking, www.vikingrange.com
Page 56 top right and bottom left: Photo courtesy of Big Chill, bigchill.com, 877-842-3269
Page 56 bottom right: Photo courtesy of Viking, www.vikingrange.com
Page 57 all: Photos courtesy of SMEG, www.smegusa.com
Page 58 top: Photo courtesy of Crown Point Cabinetry, www.crown-point.com, 800-999-4994
Page 58 bottom: Photo courtesy of Blanco America, www.blancoamerica.com
Page 59 top: Photo courtesy of Interstyle Ceramic + Glass, www.interstyle.ca, 800-944-2904
Page 59 bottom: Photo courtesy of Pyrolave, www.pyrolave.fr
Page 60 top: Photo courtesy of Blanco America, www.blancoamerica.com
Page 60 bottom left: Photo courtesy of Interstyle Ceramic + Glass, www.interstyle.ca, 800-944-2904
Page 60 bottom right: Photo courtesy of Richlite, www.richlite.com, 888-383-5533
Page 61 top: Photo courtesy of Forbo Flooring Systems, www.forbo-flooring.com
Page 61 bottom: Photo courtesy of Cosentino USA, www.silestoneusa.com, 866-268-6837
Page 62: Photo courtesy of Crown Point Cabinetry, www.crown-point.com, 800-999-4994
Page 63 left: Photo courtesy of Cambria USA, www.cambriausa.com
Page 63 right: Photo courtesy of Cosentino USA, www.silestoneusa.com, 866-268-6837
Page 64 top: Photo courtesy of Cambria USA, www.cambriausa.com
Page 64 bottom: Photo courtesy of Cosentino USA, www.silestoneusa.com, 866-268-6837
Page 65: Photo courtesy of Cosentino USA, www.silestoneusa.com, 866-268-6837
Page 66 both: Photo courtesy of Cosentino USA, www.silestoneusa.com, 866-268-6837
Page 67 top: Photo courtesy of Wilsonart International, www.wilsonart.com
Page 67 bottom: Photo courtesy of American Standard, www.americanstandard-us.com
Page 68: Photo courtesy of Formica Corporation, www.formica.com
Page 69 top: Photo courtesy of Wilsonart International, www.wilsonart.com
Page 69 bottom: Photo courtesy of Formica Corporation, www.formica.com
Page 70 both: Photo courtesy of Formica Corporation, www.formica.com
Page 71 both: Photo courtesy of Formica Corporation, www.formica.com
Page 72 top: Photo courtesy of Granite Transformations, www.granitetransformations.com
Page 72 bottom left: Photo courtesy of Urban Homes, www.uhny.com
Page 72 bottom right: Photo courtesy of Enclume, www.enclume.com, 877-362-5863
Page 73: iStock
Page 74 top: Beth Singer, photographer, www.bethsingerphotographer.com
Page 74 bottom left: Photo courtesy of DuPont Corian, www.dupont.com
Page 74 bottom right: Photo courtesy of Walker Zanger, Inc., www.walkerzanger.com
Page 75 top: Photo courtesy of Brooks Custom, www.brookscustom.com, 800-244-5432
Page 75 bottom: Photo courtesy of Brooks Custom, www.brookscustom.com, 800-244-5432
Page 76 top: Photo courtesy of Vetrazzo, www.vetrazzo.com
Page 76 bottom: Photo courtesy of J. Gleiberman Design
Page 77: Photo courtesy of Vetrazzo, www.vetrazzo.com
Page 78 left: Photo courtesy of Vetrazzo, www.vetrazzo.com
Page 78 top right: Photo courtesy of Interstyle Ceramic + Glass, www.interstyle.ca, 800-944-2904
Page 78 bottom right: Photo courtesy of Vetrazzo, www.vetrazzo.com
Page 79 top: Photo courtesy of Vetrazzo, www.vetrazzo.com
Page 79 bottom: Photo courtesy of Brooks Custom, www.brookscustom.com, 800-244-5432
Page 80: Photo courtesy of Pyrolave, www.pyrolave.fr
Page 81 both: Photo courtesy of Pyrolave, www.pyrolave.fr
Page 82 all: Photo courtesy of Brooks Custom, www.brookscustom.com, 800-244-5432
Page 83: Photo courtesy of Brooks Custom, www.brookscustom.com, 800-244-5432
Page 84 top: Photo courtesy of PanelTech/PaperStone®, www.paperstoneproducts.com, 360-538-9815
Page 84 bottom: Photo courtesy of Richlite, www.richlite.com, 888-383-5533
Page 85 top and bottom left: Photo courtesy of Richlite, www.richlite.com, 888-383-5533
Page 85 top and right: Photo courtesy of PanelTech/PaperStone®, www.paperstoneproducts.com, 360-538-9815
Page 86 top: Photo courtesy of Ikea Home Furnishings, www.ikea.com
Page 86 bottom: Todd Caverly, architectural photographer, www.toddcaverly.com

Page 87 top: Photo courtesy of Kichler Lighting, www.kichler.com, 866-558-5706
Page 87 bottom: Photo courtesy of Cambria USA, www.cambriausa.com
Page 88: Photo courtesy of GE Appliances, www.geappliances.com
Page 89 top: Photo courtesy of Blanco America, www.blancoamerica.com
Page 89 bottom: Photo courtesy of Crown Point Cabinetry, www.crown-point.com, 800-999-4994
Page 90 top: Photo courtesy of GE Appliances, www.geappliances.com
Page 90 bottom: Photo courtesy of Interstyle Ceramic + Glass, www.interstyle.ca, 800-944-2904
Page 91 top left: Photo courtesy of Interstyle Ceramic + Glass, www.interstyle.ca, 800-944-2904
Page 91 top right: Photo courtesy of Wilsonart International, www.wilsonart.com
Page 91 bottom: Photo courtesy of Interstyle Ceramic + Glass, www.interstyle.ca, 800-944-2904
Page 92 top: Photo courtesy of GE Appliances, www.geappliances.com
Page 92 bottom: Photo courtesy of LivedIn Images, www.livedinimages.com
Page 93 top left: Photo courtesy of Interstyle Ceramic + Glass, www.interstyle.ca, 800-944-2904
Page 93 bottom left: Photo courtesy of GE Appliances, www.geappliances.com
Page 93 right: Photo courtesy of Walker Zanger, Inc., www.walkerzanger.com
Page 94 top: Photo courtesy of GE Appliances, www.geappliances.com
Page 94 bottom: Photo courtesy of True Professional Series®, www.true-residential.com
Page 95: Photo courtesy of Forbo Flooring Systems, www.forbo-flooring.com
Page 96 top left: Photo courtesy of Karndean Designflooring, www.karndean.com, 886-266-4343
Page 96 top right: Photo courtesy of Armstrong Flooring, www.armstrong.com/flooring
Page 96 bottom: Photo courtesy of Karndean Designflooring, www.karndean.com, 886-266-4343
Page 97 top: Photo courtesy of Karndean Designflooring, www.karndean.com, 886-266-4343
Page 97 bottom left: Photo courtesy of Armstrong Flooring, www.armstrong.com/flooring
Page 97 bottom right: Photo courtesy of Karndean Designflooring, www.karndean.com, 886-266-4343
Page 98 top: Photo courtesy of Globus Cork, www.corkfloor.com, 718-742-7264
Page 98 bottom: Photo courtesy of Armstrong Flooring, www.armstrong.com/flooring
Page 99: Photo courtesy of Globus Cork, www.corkfloor.com, 718-742-7264
Page 100 top: Photo courtesy of Crown Point Cabinetry, www.crown-point.com, 800-999-4994
Page 100 bottom: Eric Roth, photographer, for Thomas Buekkborough, www.ericrothphoto.com
Page 101 top: Photo courtesy of Merillat, www.merillat.com
Page 101 bottom: Photo courtesy of Richlite, www.richlite.com, 888-383-5533
Page 102 both: Photos courtesy of Mirage Prefinished Hardwood Floors, www.miragefloors.com
Page 103 top: Photo courtesy of Merillat, www.merillat.com
Page 104: Photo courtesy of Canyon Creek Cabinet Company, www.canyoncreek.com
Page 105 top: Photolibrary, www.photolibrary.com
Page 105 bottom: Photo courtesy of The Solid Wood Cabinet Company, www.solidwoodcabinets.com, 855-277-4820
Page 106 top: Photo courtesy of Crown Point Cabinetry, www.crown-point.com, 800-999-4994
Page 106 bottom: Photo courtesy of The Solid Wood Cabinet Company, www.solidwoodcabinets.com, 855-277-4820
Page 107 top: Photo courtesy of Merillat, www.merillat.com
Page 107 bottom left: Photo courtesy of Kohler Plumbing, www.kohler.com
Page 107 bottom right: Photo courtesy of KraftMaid, www.kraftmaid.com
Page 108 both: Photo courtesy of Crown Point Cabinetry, www.crown-point.com, 800-999-4994
Page 109: Photo courtesy of KraftMaid, www.kraftmaid.com
Page 110 top: Photo courtesy of The Solid Wood Cabinet Company, www.solidwoodcabinets.com, 855-277-4820
Page 110 bottom: Photo courtesy of Formica Corporation, www.formica.com
Page 111 top: Photo courtesy of Plain & Fancy Custom Cabinetry, plainfancycabinetry.com
Page 111 bottom: Photo courtesy of KraftMaid, www.kraftmaid.com
Page 112 top: Photo courtesy of Kohler, www.us.kohler.com
Page 112 bottom left: Shutterstock
Page 112 bottom right: Photo courtesy of Kohler, www.us.kohler.com
Page 113 top: Photo courtesy of LivedIn Images, www.livedinimages.com
Page 113 bottom: Photo courtesy of KraftMaid, www.kraftmaid.com
Page 114: Photo courtesy of Plain & Fancy Custom Cabinetry, plainfancycabinetry.com
Page 115 all: Photo courtesy of Freedom Lift Systems, www.FreedomLiftSystems.com, 877-947-7769
Page 116 top: Photo courtesy of Merillat, www.merillat.com
Page 116 bottom left: Photo courtesy of Aristokraft Cabinetry Styles, Solutions and More, www.aristokraft.com
Page 116 bottom right: Photo courtesy of Diamond Cabinets, www.diamondcabinets.com
Page 117 top left: Photo courtesy of Merillat, www.merillat.com
Page 117 top right: Photo courtesy of Plain & Fancy Custom Cabinetry, plainfancycabinetry.com
Page 117 bottom: Photo courtesy of Merillat, www.merillat.com
Page 118 top: Photo courtesy of KraftMaid, www.kraftmaid.com
Page 118 bottom: Photo courtesy of Merillat, www.merillat.com
Page 119: Photo courtesy of Plain & Fancy Custom Cabinetry, plainfancycabinetry.com
Page 120: Photo courtesy of Merillat, www.merillat.com
Page 121 top: Photo courtesy of KraftMaid, www.kraftmaid.com
Page 121 bottom: Photo courtesy of Merillat, www.merillat.com
Page 122 top: Photo courtesy of Plain & Fancy Custom Cabinetry, plainfancycabinetry.com
Page 122 bottom: Photo courtesy of Kichler Lighting, www.kichler.com, 866-558-5706
Page 123 top: Photo courtesy of KraftMaid, www.kraftmaid.com
Page 123 bottom: Photo courtesy of True Professional Series®, www.true-residential.com
Page 124: Photo courtesy of SieMatic, www.siematic.com
Page 125 top and bottom left: Photo courtesy of Enclume, www.enclume.com, 877-362-5863
Page 125 right: iStock
Page 126 top: Photo courtesy of Ikea Home Furnishings, www.ikea.com
Page 126 bottom: Photo courtesy of Richlite, www.richlite.com, 888-383-5533

Page 127 top: Photo courtesy of Karndean Designflooring, www.karndean.com, 886-266-4343
Page 127 bottom: Photo courtesy of Interstyle Ceramic + Glass, www.interstyle.ca, 800-944-2904
Page 128: Photo courtesy of GE Appliances, www.geappliances.com
Page 129: Photo courtesy of Sub-Zero, Inc., www.subzero-wolf.com
Page 130 both: Photo courtesy of GE Appliances, www.geappliances.com
Page 131 top: Photo courtesy of GE Appliances, www.geappliances.com
Page 131 bottom: Photo courtesy of Viking, www.vikingrange.com
Page 132 top: Photo courtesy of GE Appliances, www.geappliances.com
Page 132 bottom: Shutterstock
Page 133 bottom: Photo courtesy of GE Appliances, www.geappliances.com
Page 134 top: Photo courtesy of GE Appliances, www.geappliances.com
Page 134 bottom: Photo courtesy of The Solid Wood Cabinet Company, www.solidwoodcabinets.com, 855-277-4820
Page 135 both: Photo courtesy of GE Appliances, www.geappliances.com
Page 136: Photo courtesy of Viking, www.vikingrange.com
Page 137 both: Photo courtesy of Viking, www.vikingrange.com
Page 138 top: Photo courtesy of Viking, www.vikingrange.com
Page 138 bottom: Photo courtesy of Wolf Appliance, Inc., www.subzero-wolf.com
Page 139 top: Photo courtesy of Viking, www.vikingrange.com
Page 139 bottom: Photo courtesy of Sub-Zero, Inc and Wolf Appliance, Inc., www.subzero-wolf.com
Page 140 both: Photo courtesy of True Professional Series®, www.true-residential.com
Page 141: Photo courtesy of Viking, www.vikingrange.com
Page 142 top left: Tony Giammarino, photographer, www.tonygiammarino.com
Page 142 top right: GE Appliances (General Electric), www.geappliances.com
Page 142 bottom: Photo courtesy of Plain & Fancy Custom Cabinetry, plainfancycabinetry.com
Page 143 top: Photo courtesy of Jenn-Air, jennair.com
Page 143 bottom left: GE Appliances (General Electric), www.geappliances.com
Page 143 bottom right: Photo courtesy of Eco-Timber, www.ecotimber.com
Page 144 top: Photo courtesy of Viking, www.vikingrange.com
Page 144 bottom: Photo courtesy of Walker Zanger, Inc., www.walkerzanger.com
Page 145 top: Photo courtesy of Jenn-Air, jennair.com
Page 145 bottom: Photo courtesy of Walker Zanger, Inc., www.walkerzanger.com
Page 146: Photo courtesy of American Standard, www.americanstandard-us.com
Page 147: Photo courtesy of Danze, Inc., www.danze.com
Page 148 both: Photo courtesy of American Standard, www.americanstandard-us.com
Page 149 top and bottom left: Photo courtesy of Elkay, www.elkay.com
Page 149 right: Photo courtesy of American Standard, www.americanstandard-us.com
Page 150: Photo courtesy of Elkay, www.elkay.com
Page 151 top: Photo courtesy of Danze, Inc., www.danze.com
Page 151 bottom: Photo courtesy of Blanco America, www.blancoamerica.com
Page 152 top: Photo courtesy of Danze, Inc., www.danze.com
Page 152 bottom: Photo courtesy of KraftMaid, www.kraftmaid.com
Page 153 top: Photo courtesy of Kohler, www.us.kohler.com
Page 153 bottom: Photo courtesy of American Standard, www.americanstandard-us.com
Page 154 top: Photo courtesy of American Standard, www.americanstandard-us.com
Page 154 bottom: Photo courtesy of Vetrazzo, www.vetrazzo.com
Page 155 top: Photo courtesy of Blanco America, www.blancoamerica.com
Page 155 bottom: Photo courtesy of Elkay, www.elkay.com
Page 156 both: Photo courtesy of Kohler, www.us.kohler.com
Page 157: Photo courtesy of Blanco America, www.blancoamerica.com
Page 158: Photo courtesy of Crown Point Cabinetry, www.crown-point.com, 800-999-4994
Page 159 top left: Photo courtesy of Merillat, www.merillat.com
Page 159 bottom left: Photo courtesy of Elkay, www.elkay.com
Page 159 right: Photo courtesy of Vetrazzo, www.vetrazzo.com
Page 160 top: Photo courtesy of Crown Point Cabinetry, www.crown-point.com, 800-999-4994
Page 160 bottom: Photo courtesy of Blanco America, www.blancoamerica.com
Page 161: Photo courtesy of Pottery Barn, potterybarn.com, 888-779-5176
Page 162: Photo courtesy of GE Appliances, www.geappliances.com
Page 163: Shutterstock
Page 164 top: Photo courtesy of Viking, www.vikingrange.com
Page 164 bottom left: Photo courtesy of Kohler Plumbing, www.kohler.com
Page 164 bottom right: Photo courtesy of Ikea, www.ikea.com
Page 165 top: Photo courtesy of Kichler Lighting, www.kichler.com, 866-558-5706
Page 165 bottom: Photo courtesy of Solatube, www.solatube.com, 888-SOLATUBE
Page 166: Shutterstock
Page 167 top: Photo courtesy of Crown Point Cabinetry, www.crown-point.com, 800-999-4994
Page 167 bottom: Photo courtesy of Kichler Lighting, www.kichler.com, 866-558-5706
Page 168 left: Photo courtesy of Cambria Natural Quartz Countertops, www.cambriausa.com
Page 168 top right: Photo courtesy of tiella, www.tiella.com
Page 168 bottom right: Photo courtesy of Juno Lighting Group, www.junolightinggroup.com
Page 169 top: Photo courtesy of Kichler Lighting, www.kichler.com, 866-558-5706
Page 169 bottom left: Photo courtesy of Interstyle Ceramic + Glass, www.interstyle.ca, 800-944-2904
Page 169 bottom right: Photo courtesy of Interstyle Ceramic + Glass, www.interstyle.ca, 800-944-2904
Page 170 top: Photo courtesy of Kichler Lighting, www.kichler.com, 866-558-5706
Page 170 bottom: Photo courtesy of DeWitt Designer Kitchens, www.dewittdesignerkitchens.com, (626) 792-8833
Page 171: Photo courtesy of Kichler Lighting, www.kichler.com, 866-558-5706
Page 172: Photo courtesy of Karndean Designflooring, www.karndean.com, 886-266-4343
Page 173 all: Photo courtesy of Blanco America, www.blancoamerica.com
Page 174 top left: Photo courtesy of Enclume, www.enclume.com, 877-362-5863
Page 174 top right: Photo courtesy of Elkay, www.elkay.com
Page 174 bottom left: Photo courtesy of Top Knobs, www.topknobs.com
Page 174 bottom right: Photo courtesy of KraftMaid, www.kraftmaid.com

Resources

American Standard
Faucets, sinks, and accessories.
www.americanstandard-us.com

Anvil Motion
Universal Design automated cabinetry.
www.anvilmotion.com

Big Chill
Colored appliances and fixtures.
www.bigchill.com
(877) 842-3269

Blanco America
Sinks, faucets, and accessories.
www.blancoamerica.com

Bosch
Kitchen appliances and ventilation.
www.bosch-home.com/us/

Cambria
Quartz countertops.
www.cambriausa.com

Canyon Creek Cabinetry
Custom cabinetry.
www.canyoncreek.com
(800) 228-1830

Crown Point Cabinetry
Custom cabinetry.
www.crown-point.com
(800) 999-4994

Elkay Manufacturing Company
Sinks, faucets, and accessories.
www.elkayusa.com

Globus Cork Flooring
Cork flooring.
www.corkfloor.com
(718) 742-7264

Forbo
Marmoleum Click flooring.
www.forbo.com

Formica
Laminate countertops.
www.formica.com

KraftMaid
A full range of cabinetry and cabinetry accessories.
www.kraftmaid.com
(888) 562-7744

Merillat
A full range of cabinetry and cabinetry accessories.
www.merillat.com
(866) 850-8557

National Kitchen & Bath Association
Kitchen planning advice and guidance, listings or professionals, design idea guides.
www.nkba.org
(800) 843-6522

PaperStone
Recycled paper countertops.
www.paperstoneproducts.com
(360) 538-1480

RichLite
Recycled paper countertops.
www.richlite.com
(888) 383-5533

Silestone
Quartz countertops.
www.silestoneusa.com
(866) 268-6837

SMEG
Italian-designed appliances.
www.smegusa.com
(866) 736-7634

Sub-Zero
High-end, restaurant quality appliances.
www.subzero-wolf.com

Vetrazzo
Recycled glass countertops.
www.vetrazzo.com

Viking
High-end, restaurant quality appliances.
www.vikingrange.com

WalkerZanger
Ceramic and stone tile.
www.walkerzanger.com

WilsonArt
Laminate and solid-surface countertops and flooring products.
http://www.wilsonart.com

Mokena Community
Public Library District